Managing
Your
Escape

DRAWINGS BY Susan LeVan

Managing Your Escape

TAKING CARE OF PERSONAL BUSINESS SO YOU CAN GET AWAY

BY Katy Burke

SEVEN SEAS PRESS, INC., NEWPORT, R.I.

DEDICATION
To June MacQuarrie and Ed LaVigueur,
who have it all together.

Published by Seven Seas Press, Inc., Newport, Rhode Island 02840
Edited by James R. Gilbert

Library of Congress Cataloging in Publication Data

Burke, Katy.
 Managing your escape.

 1. Finance, Personal.   2. Life skills.   3. Escape
(Psychology)   I. Title.
HG179.B834   647.7   83-20258
ISBN 0-915160-67-6

Book trade distribution by Simon and Schuster, a division of Simon and Schuster, Inc. 1230 Avenue of the Americas, New York, NY 10020

Designed by Irving Perkins Associates
Illustrations by Susan LeVan
Printed in the United States of America

Contents

Acknowledgments

No book is written entirely alone, especially one of this genre. Well, the actual putting down of words is a solitary pursuit, but many people contributed to producing this one, either with support and encouragement or with the sharing of knowledge and experience, or all of the above.

Taz Waller was my mainstay. He would come home from a long day at work, put dinner on, feed the cat and pour the wine so we could relax in the cockpit, talk and watch the sunset. He listened endlessly to my ideas and occasional rantings. He gave suggestions, reassurance and solace.

As with the first book, those at Seven Seas, Jim Gilbert and Andrew Rock, provided invaluable assistance with new ideas, concrete suggestions, good editing and an objective outlook. And Kim Spruance did an outstanding job of typing page after page of manuscript.

Long-distance cruisers, several of whom have completed circumnavigations, were especially helpful in offering advice and information on how they handled business matters in foreign countries. Special thanks go to Lin and Larry Pardey, Sy and Vicki Carkhuff, Earl Hinz and Wayne Carpenter. They shared that particular kind of knowledge that only can come from having "been there".

Other cruisers and sailors who shared cruising experiences and sometimes expertise in related fields include Bob and Shearlean Duke, Jack and Pat Tyler, Gainor Roberts, George Cranston, Bob Vollmer, Dick and Karen Brashear, Donald Street, Steve Bloch, Chereese Smoot, Lorin Weiss, Lew and Kim Spruance, and Mark and Christi Paulus.

Many professional people who were not sailors helped, too, of course: stockbrokers, investment counselors, bankers, insurance agents. While I couldn't begin to list them all by name, I must mention investment counselor Rick Liebley, stockbroker Mike Nader and Joan Curtis, good friend as well as my accountant. They all spent long hours explaining their particular fields and going over parts of this manuscript.

And, though I've already mentioned her, an extra thank you to an extraordinary woman. Lin Pardey would come roaring "down from the mountain" in a battered old pickup truck to run errands, pick up parts for *Taleisin*, the boat she and Larry are building, and join me for lunch. Her encouragement and her unfailing good humor were often just the needed catalyst to keep me going.

Introduction

When my editor Jim Gilbert first approached me about doing a book on how to get your act together to take off on an extended escape, I though he was a little daft. To be specific, I thought he'd gone completely off the deep end. Me? The original get-a-nickel, spend-a-nickel kid? Financial planning? "Well, think about it," said Jim.

I did think about it—a lot—and decided perhaps I *was* a good choice to write this book. It's true I am neither a banker, stockbroker nor accountant. But then professional people tend to have narrow outlooks, seeing only the parameters of their own fields. More than anything else, I decided, this book required the energies of a generalist, particularly one who has made numerous escapes herself.

What I am is a cruising sailor (also a naval architect and a writer). A great part of my last seven years have been spent voyaging on sailboats. And, from time to time, I've even found it necessary to make an escape to the mountains if, for no other reason, just to be alone. So, while I'm not a professional in any of the estate planning fields, I have acquired a great deal of experience in the art of escape. And while my own passion is sailing off to the far horizon in sailboats, much of what I learned is applicable to any kind of escape, be it by camper, recreational vehicle, backpack, motorcycle, airplane or hot-air balloon.

And then it came to me that I'm not the only person I know who's skilled in the art of "escape management." After all, cruising sailors have been doing it for years. In the process of my own cruising I've met, quite literally, many hundreds of fellow cruisers on their own escapes, some young, others elderly, some skilled, some not, some rich and some owning only the boat under their feet and the shirts on their backs. Many of those I've met along the way became fast friends. Together, I thought, we probably know as much about the art of making a successful getaway as any identifiable group in Western Civilization. I have counted heavily on their experience.

But I also interviewed scores of professional people, bankers, investment counselors, stockbrokers, insurance brokers, accountants, doctors, lawyers, educators, career counselors, some sailors, some not. They all took an interest in this project—perhaps because the dream of escaping it all touches everyone at one time or another. These professionals gave me many hours of their valuable time.

Perhaps a few words are in order about what this book is *not* about. It's not about how to get rich quick (or at all). It's not about how to make a killing in the stock market. It's not even about how to support yourself if you choose to take off on a dream and a promise without a dime in your pocket. Such frugal escapes have been done, yes, and I do mention some ways you can supplement your income along the way—but that's not my primary focus.

I assume you have some money, not a lot, but some; at least the escape kitty has been started. If you can afford to cruise in the style of William F. Buckley, with a steward to make down your bunk every night and lay out a fresh shirt each morning, you probably won't find this book of much use. Most of us go in a simpler, less expensive way. The most-asked questions by those people I have met who would like to take off for the distant horizon deal with the same subject: money. For the most part, that's what the book is about. Money. And planning, since the two so often go hand in hand.

One subject suggested early-on by Jim that we eventually rejected was a chapter called, "Who Can Go." It's too negative. Who can go implies somehow there are those who cannot. And I think everyone can. You may choose not to for any number of reasons, but if you really want to escape, you can and you will.

An artful escape—one that lets you "go where you want to go, do what you want to do," as the old "The Mamas and Papas" tune said —takes a lot of planning and it takes some money. But it can and is being done every day.

I like to think this book will help you make that dream cruise or ultimate escape, whatever and wherever that is. Instead of worrying about finances after you leave, worry about them now. Not only will it be easier to make the break, but it will help you enjoy your adventure of a lifetime once it's no longer a dream.

And when you're out there, living your escape, I hope your biggest decision for the day is whether to stay at anchor and dive for lobster or hoist sail in the warm trades to move on to another port.

Katy Burke
aboard *Alliance*
Newport Beach, California

CHAPTER ONE

Making the Big Decisions

Set goals but not deadlines

A friend of mine is fond of saying, "Everything is permanent until further notice." She's usually referring to husbands, but it can apply just as easily to making an escape.

Just the decision *to* escape is monumental, to say nothing of all the decisions that follow. Don't let the idea of making a getaway scare you. It doesn't have to be a total, irreversible commitment. It does, however, take a certain amount of drive and singlemindedness to take care of the hundred and one little details of a business and personal nature that demand attention before you can sail off into the sunset. Also, these details don't all have to be done at once. Indeed, you're much better off taking your time. If you have the luxury of time, use it.

 **Don't let the idea of escape scare you. It doesn't have to be a total, irreversible commitment.**

More than once I've seen someone decide to go cruising, my favorite form of escape. They set a departure date and then go absolutely bonkers trying to keep the date. Forget it! The scheming, the planning, the shared evenings (if more than one soul is in on the escape) even the drudge work—such as readying the boat—should all be enjoyable experiences. The planning, too, is a part of the artful escape. Become a slave to a rigid schedule and much of the joy will disappear.

Set goals, absolutely, but realize that it's not the end of the world if a deadline is missed. And don't ever announce a departure date to friends and family. Without intending to, they can heap an enormous amount of pressure on you. After a while, remarks such as, "How come you're still here? I thought you were going cruising?" can really set your teeth on edge.

When I first met Dick and Helen Pentoney and their daughter Valarie, they were getting ready for a cruise around the world. The previous five years had been spent getting ready: living aboard, making innumerable modifications to *Heron*, provisioning, and all the while cruising the eastern seaboard. Dick told me he got so tired of being asked why they hadn't left yet he finally refused to talk to anyone about it. "When we're ready" became his pat reply. They delayed for another full year, but they *did* go, to the amazement of skeptics along the dock who thought the Pentoneys would spend forever getting ready.

 **Even the planning should be part of a joyous escape. But become a slave to a rigid escape schedule, and much of the joy will disappear.**

One Day At a Time

Most escapes, except perhaps those from the long arm of the law, are not for a lifetime. Most sailing escapes begin with a definite time frame, a year or two perhaps, sometimes as long as five or six. The fact that so many decide to keep going after the initial period ends is proof that cruising *is* one great way to live.

Be realistic in your escape plans. In the case of those who want to make their getaway by sea, for example, the amount of previous sailing/cruising will be a major influence in their where-to-go and for-how-long decisions. Anyone who's only done a little weekend sailing would be foolish to buy a large boat, equip it for ocean work (assuming he would even know how to do that) and head out for the south seas. It's been done, yes, but at great risk and only with a lot of luck.

It's better to take it slow. Spend a year or so living aboard and cruising locally. Get to know your boat, camper or other escape vehicle. Take it easy and slow so you don't bite off too much, too soon. If you're going to escape to a log cabin in the north woods, spend some time there beforehand. You may find it difficult to write poetry by candlelight or to cart around your easel in snowshoes.

In the case of sailing escapes, many people find they don't enjoy offshore cruising anyway. But that doesn't stop them from taking off. I know several California sailors who wanted to cruise the U.S. East

Coast, the Bahamas, and/or the Caribbean. Most of them had done some cruising in Mexico and while they enjoyed that, they had no desire to sail all the way to the Panama Canal, either by going offshore several hundred miles or by sailing closer-in along the troublesome Central American coasts. Instead, they chose to have the boat trucked to Texas, where they could cruise at far less the cost of equipping and provisioning for a passage around via the Canal.

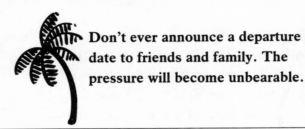 **Don't ever announce a departure date to friends and family. The pressure will become unbearable.**

No matter what type of escape appeals to you, or what length of time will be allotted, several big items will require some thoughtful attention before a realistic escape plan can be hatched.

Paying Off the Escape Vehicle

Throughout this book, the assumption is made that the boat or other means of getaway is paid for: you own her free and clear. If you don't, I recommend that getting those payments out of the way become the number one priority. Notice in the budget chapter that no provision is made for monthly escape vehicle payments in the chart of typical expenses. If these payments were included, monthly expenses could easily rise by 40% or 50%, even more when we consider that a financed boat or camper must be insured. The fact is that the vast majority of people doing extended cruising are doing so in boats that are paid for. Otherwise, they couldn't afford to go.

Paying for a big piece of equipment such as a boat or a camper is never easy. And the prospect of buying it, then taking 15 years to pay it off, is hardly appealing; not if it means putting off your escape for 15 years. One alternative is to finance for fewer years, which will mean higher monthly payments but the pain will be over sooner. Or buy an older, less expensive escape vehicle that can be paid for more readily.

Many sailors are able to sell some sizable holding—like a house—to pay for their boat.

Some financial institutions include a prepayment penalty on boat loans and loans for other recreational vehicles. If you are about to shop for a loan, make very sure that it does not carry a penalty for paying off early or for making payments ahead of schedule. You definitely want the option of paying off the loan as fast as possible, without being penalized for it.

Some people work hard and double up on payments, or save until they have enough to prepay the loan for a specific length of time—a summer or possibly a year or longer. If you want to try this, talk to your loan officer first. Make very sure that any prepayments come off the front of the loan and not from the end. If an extra payment on a ten-year loan will be considered as the 120th, it's not going to be of any value if your plans are for the coming summer.

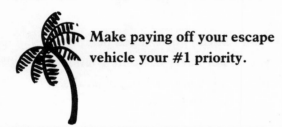

Make paying off your escape vehicle your #1 priority.

Anyone planning on cruising and making loan payments at the same time should keep in mind that they can only cruise to the navigational limits of their insurance policy (see the chapter on boat insurance). The same applies for owners of recreational vehicles. While an insurance company may be willing to write coverage for more distant ports, it will be a lot tougher to convince your friendly banker that you are neither about to skip out on the loan nor sail off into unknown territory and drive your boat or camper off the edge of the world. Until the boat is owned free and clear, the banker *does* have a stake in the investment just as you do. And, unfortunately, he does have a right to say where it can and cannot go.

Handling the Job

One of the high points of leaving may be walking into the boss' office and telling him precisely what he can do with the job you've slaved away at for years. Don't be hasty. There may be some good reasons for *not* quitting, at least not right away. If there is any chance at all you might be returning some day, think about taking a leave of absence, at least for the first year. Or think about requesting a sabbatical leave for a year or so (more on this in Chapter Two).

By the end of the first year, you will have a much better idea of how you feel about your escape and will know exactly where you want to spend the *next* year. If you're sailing, you may decide that you want to keep cruising, and the best way to do that is to go back to your old job for awhile because that's the fastest way to make the kind of money to let you cruise longer and further the next time. A leave of absence will, in most instances, allow you to retain seniority and step back in at a good pay rate, rather than starting out as a new employee somewhere else, likely at a lower salary.

 **Don't burn your bridges behind you. There may be some sound reasons for not quitting even the most humdrum job.**

I remember meeting a couple—both college professors—who were on a year's sabbatical, cruising to the Caribbean with their two teen-age children. Judy told me they had decided to cruise now, rather than wait for retirement, because they wanted to share the experience as a family. If they waited, the kids would be grown and out on their own, not likely to be interested in spending a year with Mom and Dad —even on a boat. The sabbatical allowed them to retain all vested rights and seniority. They felt secure in knowing they could return to their old positions and continue to support themselves and their children.

Another reason for taking a leave of absence is that it may enable you to continue health insurance or other benefits at group rates—or allow you to keep your retirement fund intact. Check out all the possibilities before handing in that letter of resignation.

The House: Sell or Rent?

One of the homeowner's biggest decisions is whether or not to sell the house. It is a major investment, so it's a major decision. One very good reason for selling the house is to pay for the boat (or any other major escape expense, such as airfare). That's exactly what many cruisers do. Keep in mind, however, that capital gains tax may have to be paid on any profit. If your boat, camper or RV will become your principal residence, tax laws will apply to its purchase just as if you were reinvesting in another house. To determine how your own finances would be affected—and before making a final decision to put the house on the market—spend some time with your tax adviser or accountant. And get a copy of Publication 523, "Tax Information on Selling Your Home," from a local IRS office. Someone who is quitting work to go cruising and will then be in a lower tax bracket may find it's better to postpone the sale for a year or two.

Others sell their house, not to pay for the boat, but to pay for the cruise itself. By investing the money in stocks, bonds, a money market fund or an interest-bearing bank account, they can cruise comfortably with a secure, steady income (more on this topic in Chapter Six).

Good reasons exist, however, for keeping the house, particularly if the escape machine is paid for. Renting the house should cover monthly payments and property taxes (and might even add to the cruising fund), while equity will continue to grow. It's an important consideration for those who plan on returning to shore life in a year or two. Property values and interest rates rarely go down and the replacement cost for a house of similar value when you return could be high enough to place it out of reach.

If you've owned the house for a long time, chances are the payments are low, probably much lower than its rental value. I know several couples who are cruising on money coming primarily from rental income. Their only worry is that the tenants will move out and the house will sit vacant. A month-to-month rental is not a good idea for an absentee owner. It's better to have a lease, and require the first and last month's rent in advance, so there's a cushion in case the tenants do decide to move.

If the house is almost paid for, it can be viewed as a long-term source of income. And some simply feel more comfortable about leaving if they still have a home to which they can return.

 **If your house is paid for, it can pay for your escape for years to come.**

The Car: Sell it or Store it?

Selling the car (or cars) is one decision that most of us make very easily. Indeed, it's often more than just getting rid of a big expense: it's a symbolic gesture, proof that we have cut the ties and are truly "on our way." About the only reason for keeping a car is if it is paid for and the escape is to be short—a summer perhaps. Make arrangements with someone trustworthy to drive it and pay for the insurance and upkeep, or better yet, put it in storage. Unless it goes in a relative's garage, you'll have the additional expense of a monthly storage bill. Consult with a mechanic to determine the best way of storing a car so it will be in good shape on your return.

I do know a few people who kept a car while they were coastal cruising. They would sail into a port and decide to stay for awhile. Someone would then get on the bus, return to the last port and retrieve the car. While they never seemed to have any trouble finding a place to leave it, the whole operation always appeared to be more trouble than it was worth.

I haven't owned a car in more than nine years, and have managed to get around just fine: by walking, bike riding or using public transportation. The cost of an occasional taxi (usually when it's pouring rain) is miniscule compared to the expense of car ownership. My boatmate Taz needs a car now to drive to work, but you can bet it will be the first thing sold when we go cruising.

 **About the only reason for keeping your car is if it's paid for and you're only leaving for a short time.**

A car is one item that *is* easy to replace should you decide to come back to shore life. Most of the cruising people I know don't seem as emotionally attached to their cars as shore people. And the ones who do buy cars on their return seldom buy a new one; they view it as transportation, and nothing more.

Dealing with Personal Treasures

We may or may not have emotional ties to our cars, but personal possessions—books, paintings, souvenirs, trinkets of all kinds—are a different story. Deciding what to do with these items is often hardest because they do have emotional, instead of purely practical, value.

Furniture (except for antiques) and household items, such as blenders and electric can openers, always can be replaced. But don't be too hasty about getting rid of personal treasures that are irreplaceable. Start telling a spouse that he or she must give up everything that won't fit on the boat, and you're liable to have more trouble than you thought possible.

It's too big a trauma to get rid of everything all at once. Weed through possessions slowly, selling, trading or giving away a little at a time. Going slowly is also good insurance against ridding yourself of items below their market value. Sometimes it helps to think positively about family treasures. For instance, you may own an old violin that once belonged to your grandfather. You know it's worth some money. But you never play it. It sits in the closet gathering dust. No one else in the family gives a hoot about it. But still, it did belong to Grandpa and you can't quite give it up. Don't think of it as selling Grandpa's violin; think of it as buying a new family treasure, say, a new VHF radio or a chiming ship's clock. And when you do sell it, go buy the clock or the radio—right now.

Another idea that often seems to help is to give special possessions to special friends—to someone who will treasure them and appreciate them the way you do. You'll know you can see them again whenever you pay a visit. I owned a massive library of hardbound books. Only an armload could go on the boat. I valued that collection highly (and still do) and couldn't bear the thought of never seeing it again. I gave it to some close friends who feel the way I do about books. When I get back for a visit, it makes me feel good to see all those volumes on the shelves in Willie's study, and to know they are being used.

Items such as books, paintings and art objects, can sometimes be donated to libraries, museums or schools and then used as a tax deduction. Depending on your tax bracket, this could be more advantageous than simply selling everything.

 Get rid of personal treasures slowly. And never attempt telling your spouse what he/she should be rid of.

After all the sorting-out process is over, there is still likely to be a big pile of stuff that you simply cannot part with. So *don't*. Keep it. Pack it away somewhere safe, even if it means renting storage space. If your escape lasts for many years you will, eventually, get rid of it. But don't do it until it can be done painlessly.

When I first went cruising, I left an attic full of treasures at the home of some friends. Two years later they got divorced and sold the house. After paying for a plane ticket to fly back and rescue my belongings, I was much more objective about their value. I even sold enough to almost cover the cost of the trip. And it was interesting to discover how many things I had completely forgotten about. Three days of weeding out reduced the bulk to a size that would fit into a 3' x 3' x 8' storage locker—at a cost of $150 a year. Now, finally, that treasure trove has been reduced to one cardboard box in my aunt's garage. Funny, but I can't think of one thing that's in the box.

Personal belongings are the hardest to part with. I don't regret taking so long to get rid of what I did, and I don't mind the money I spent on airfare or locker rent. Had I decided at any point over the years to stop cruising, I would have been very glad to have what was left. Now enough time has passed and my attitude has changed enough because of the cruising lifestyle that those "treasures" have no meaning. Were I to move ashore now, I wouldn't want them. If any of it did have meaning I would still have it, storage fees and all.

Now I wonder what's in the last box that's so important?

CHAPTER TWO

Keeping the Resume Spotless

How to Escape and Keep Your Status, Too

It may strike you as odd that this chapter, which deals with returning from the ultimate escape, is positioned near the beginning of this book.

Anyone can make their escape by simply getting up, casting fate to the wind and taking off for the distant horizon. But the *art* of escaping ensures that, with a little planning, your options at escape's end are just as plentiful—perhaps even more so—than they are now.

Is There Really Such a Thing as Security?

One worry that many people have, indeed one that keeps quite a few from ever going cruising, is that of quitting a secure job and then reentering the job market on their return. It *is* a risk, but then no job is completely secure. There are no guarantees that a job will last forever or that a business won't fail. Well, a Supreme Court justice may have more job security than most, but times change and life is full of surprises.

 **The art of escaping means planning** ***today*** **to keep** ***tomorrow's*** **options plentiful.**

I knew a juvenile court judge in Southern California. His boat was fully equipped and ready for cruising and he wanted to go; it was an all-consuming passion and the only subject he ever talked about. But his job was so secure! He knew if he could just "hang on" and stick it out for another 12 years he could retire and cruise with a comfortable, dependable monthly income. The waiting was tearing him apart, but he just couldn't let go of that security blanket. His friends watched him agonize. I figured he would die of a stroke long before he ever reached retirement age.

Then the voters of California passed Proposition 13, forcing all government agencies to tighten their belts. Fred had the least seniority and, to the amazement of all, lost his job. He immediately moved aboard the boat (to save money) and took a low-paying summer job with a sailmaker to learn some basic sewing skills, ones he thought might come in handy later on.

That was several years ago. He did go cruising. In fact, he's still cruising. He shipped the boat east, and now works summers in boat yards to pay for winter cruising in the Bahamas: And, yes, he does pick up odd jobs here and there doing canvas work and sail repairs. He still talks about "maybe" going back into law practice somewhere, or "maybe" doing something else. But right now he is content with the cruising life. He has lost his 20 pounds of potbelly, is tan and healthy, and I have never seen him so relaxed and happy.

Luckily, attitudes are starting to change and the old concept of the "company man" is on its way out. It is seldom expected anymore that someone will graduate from college, join a corporation and remain a loyal, steadfast employee until retirement. Instead, the expectation now is that an executive will change companies at least three or four times, and probably more often on his or her way to the top. It's becoming more common, too, for people to change their entire careers, not just switch companies, once or twice during their lifetime.

 **The old "company man" concept is on its way out. It's not uncommon today to change jobs— even careers—several times during one's working lifetime.**

Planning Today for Tomorrow's Resume

But even for the most highly skilled people, an escape poses an interesting problem. How would a resume look with the line, "June 1979–April 1982: unemployed, went sailing"? It does sound a little flaky, doesn't it?

Career consultant Marty Verboon agreed that it could indicate a "lack of stability." But she also said if a resume is worded correctly

—and good reasons are given for taking the time off—it might not be detrimental. A paragraph about meeting challenges, increasing one's confidence, learning self-reliance, the broadening effects of travel, or working together as a family unit all have a better ring than simply, "got tired of my humdrum existence, wanted to get away for awhile."

Another career counselor, Lou Samuels, said he had found employment for several people who had taken a year or longer off work—for personal reasons—including one person who went cruising and another executive who spent a year and a half doing oil painting and photography while living in a secluded mountain cabin. Samuels said the time they had taken off was a definite plus when they returned to work. He believed it showed they were flexible, forward-thinking and aggressive, people in charge of their lives and people who would be an asset in today's modern corporate structure. He said he had no trouble finding employment for any of them!

 **Taking time off to escape the humdrum life doesn't have to show as a void on your resume. It can also prove you are flexible and forward-thinking—an asset to today's modern corporation.**

It is a good idea for any professional who normally finds employment through an agency to talk with a career counselor *before* leaving, or *before* quitting their job. A counselor who understands your particular field (computers, financing, marketing, etc.) will know the ins and outs of job hunting and may be able to offer suggestions that will smooth the way when you return. For instance, if you are working in a field of rapidly-changing technology where it is important to keep abreast of new developments, a counselor might suggest keeping up subscriptions to trade journals. You may be "away", but you won't have been "out of it."

In other cases, a counselor may feel it will be necessary to enroll in one or two college courses to catch up before reentering the job market, particularly if you are going away for several years. *Now* is the time to find out if such possibilities exist, so plans can be made ahead and so you'll have fewer surprises when the escape is over.

After discussions with personnel directors at large and small companies as well as career consultants and employment agencies, it is clear that various factors enter into a hire/not hire decision:

- REASONS FOR THE TIME OFF: This is important to everyone. Make it good, even if it's mostly a lot of bull. Women, particulary, can sometimes use the ploy, "Well, it's something my husband has wanted to do for years, and this seemed like the ideal time for it . . ." Unfortunately, it's a little harder for a man to say his wife wanted to cruise and he went along to please her—even though that sometimes is the case. Careers in certain fields are definitely enhanced by travel/cruising, such as the boating industry, the travel industry, journalism and education.

 **Talk to a career counselor *before* you take off or quit your existing job.**

- QUALIFICATIONS: The better someone is at what they do, the easier it will be to find work when they return, even if they've spent the past few years sailing a boat or living in a grass shack. Those without skills will have just as hard a time finding a good job when they get back as they would have had they remained ashore.
- PAST EXPERIENCE: This goes hand-in-hand with qualifications. Prospective employers always want to know where an applicant has worked, for how long, and what his/her responsibilities were. A history of good, steady employment can go a long way towards offsetting any negative attitudes about your getaway interlude.
- THE TRACK RECORD: While a few people said it mattered that someone dropped out of the work force for a while, most *did* say it would make a difference if it happened repeatedly. Working a few years, cruising a few years, working a few years,

cruising a few years, etc., does not demonstrate stability or permanence. Many people, however do exactly that for years. But the *type* of work is what makes the difference. Waiting on tables, working in boat yards, taking summer jobs in resort areas all are transient employment. These employers don't expect their workers to hang around forever. But corporations looking to fill management-level positions want to believe that whoever they hire is planning on making a career. One sabbatical may be acceptable, but here today, gone tomorrow is not.

 **A history of successful, steady employment goes a long way toward offsetting any negative attitudes about your escape.**

Working on the Go at Good Jobs

Some professions do lend themselves to temporary labor. A prime example is the electronics industry. Many draftsmen, designers and engineers earn top wages working for "job shops" instead of directly for a company. They may work for several months or several years to complete a project, then move on to another job at a different company. Going to another city or taking off for a few years makes little difference if they are highly qualified.

Other occupations are so short in skilled people that a trained professional can find work just about anywhere. Nurses and medical technicians, for instance, always seem to find employment easily.

Not every employer, of course, is going to welcome you with open arms. Large established corporations are generally more rigid in their outlook and their expectations than are smaller, younger companies. Large firms are more apt to have dress codes, rigid hierarchy, a fixed "mold" into which each employee is supposed to fit. Be prepared for the occasional stuffed shirt who will look with shock and possible anger at any person who would dare to deviate from the norm in such a manner. "Cruising? In a little boat? Not working for a living? We don't hire weirdos, my friend!" But then, would you want to work for such a company anyway? I rather doubt it.

I recently called a woman with whom I had worked years ago. I quit one day, threw away my dresses and nylons and went to work cleaning, painting and varnishing boats. I went on to become a naval architect and then a writer. Jan went on to become director of customer relations for a large electronics firm in Northern California, with 30 employees in her charge.

"Jan," I asked her, "if I decided to settle down and go back to work at a 'real' job and met your qualifications, would you hire me?"

"Not a chance," she replied.

That took me aback. "Why not?" I demanded.

"Well," she said, "I wouldn't want to say you're unstable, but you've just been out of it too long. You wouldn't be happy here. You might like it at first because it would be something new and different, but then you'd get bored. You'd go into culture shock. I wouldn't give it six months before you'd be off again."

She's right, of course.

 **Be prepared for stuffed shirts who would be shocked by anyone who would want to leave the workaday life, even on a temporary escape. But would you want to work for them, anyway?**

The lesson is, before making your escape, plan for an eventual return, whether it's a fixed date or some vague point in the future. Think about where and how you might want to live, what kind of work you might like to do. But know that it's all subject to change, and prepare for *that* eventuality, too. You may return and find that the world hasn't changed at all—politicians are still making promises they'll never keep, prices are still too high at the supermarket, rush-hour traffic is still snaking along the freeway, cousin Sally is still getting a new permanent-wave every six months and the school board is still feuding over sex education for ten-year-olds. But *you* will have changed, and you'll be the better for it.

CHAPTER THREE

Budgeting Your Resources

Learning to Live with Less

For the majority of people making escapes, the new lifestyle includes learning to live on a reduced income. Some have taken an early retirement at a reduction of their previous salaries. Others save up until they have enough to take off for a year or two, or "until the money runs out."

Most of us find the rewards of an escape so great that it doesn't seem like a hardship at all to give up some of the old luxuries, like tickets to the hottest new Broadway play or dinners at the fanciest seafood restaurant in town. Who needs the seafood restaurant when we can dive for lobster on a Caribbean reef or spend a lazy morning gathering mussels or digging for clams along a quiet stretch of Cape Cod shore?

Then, too, some of the old expenses are reduced—often drastically. A good example of this is clothes. The executive who spent a fortune every year on Brooks Brothers suits and a closet full of white shirts switches to cut-off jeans, scruffy deck shoes and a healthy suntan. That's a bit of a savings right there. Add up just how much you spend a year for the pleasure of driving a car (payment, insurance, gas, oil, repairs) and right there is several thousand dollars you'll no longer spend.

Obviously, there is no quick and easy answer to the question about how much it costs to escape. A cruising sailor will spend less on housing and transportation during the escape but, of course, he had to spend more up front to buy the boat. The same is true for someone escaping in any other form of live-aboard vehicle. More on this question later in this chapter.

I know what it costs me and I know what it costs some other cruisers. The truth is, everybody does it differently. My first year cruising and living aboard in New England, my shipmate and I survived on about $200 a month. That same year, another couple left on a round-the-world passage. They reported managing just fine on $1,800 a month. A big part of the difference is they traveled inland extensively (by plane, train or rented car) in every country they visited.

Another factor that can make a difference between cruisers (and campers) is dockage. Some use free stopping places virtually all the time. Cost: zero or close to it. Others go dockside (or use camp-grounds) every chance they get. Cost: anywhere from $100 to $500 a month, depending on the area. Other factors are how often you eat out or catch fish; whether you drink and/or smoke; whether you frequent local bistros or watch sunsets. It all makes a difference.

But with some careful record-keeping and a realistic analysis of what you can and cannot live without, it is possible to project how much you're going to need. And if the bottom line looks scary, re-member this: just about everyone lives to their limits. One cruiser I know has an inheritance that gives her $2,000 every month. She spends it all, beer for the boys at the bar, steak and eggs for breakfast and fancy paint jobs for the boat. Another couple figured they could cruise for two years if they kept expenses at $300 a month. They succeeded, but only with what many people would consider a lot of sacrifices. The commitment and determination was there or they never would have made it.

Getting-Ready Expenses

It may be possible to live pretty inexpensively once the escape begins, but you can count on spending a bundle of money *before* you leave. And the farther away you plan on going, the more you are likely to spend up front. A boat, for example, can sit in a slip for years, just going out for occasional weekend trips. She requires only routine maintenance and a certain amount of equipment to make her a com-fortable retreat. If a fitting breaks or the cook runs out of paper plates, a quick trip to the neighborhood store will take care of it.

But when cruising, there won't always be a neighborhood store, and if there is, it may not have what you're looking for. The cruising boat—and to a lesser extent most land-based escape vehicles—is a well-stocked, self-contained environment that gives its crew the free-dom and self-sufficiency to go where they want when they want. A cruising sailor is more apt to visit his spare parts locker than a hard-ware store to replace a broken shackle or to get a new tube of grease for the winch. Few things are more frustrating than watching weeks of perfect sailing weather slip by while being stuck at a dock waiting for the plane to land bringing a "must have" part from the repair shop back home. It's better to have those parts aboard, particularly if you're not super-adept at improvising. Don't worry, after cruising awhile, you will be!

I once knew a guy who owned two Morgan automobiles, one to drive and one for spare parts. While not suggesting taking off on one boat or camper and towing another for spare parts, the more spares you can reasonably carry, the more self-sufficient you'll be.

For just about everyone, myself included, the very first "getting ready" expenditure cost less than $3.00. It's a notebook. A notebook that gets filled with lists and lists and more lists.

Try to make a realistic analysis of how much money you will need on your escape. But remember, just about everyone lives to their financial limits. You'll have no more trouble spending $2,000 a month than $300.

- EQUIPMENT: This could be a long list. My own includes such boat items as a ham radio, a salt water pump for the galley, storm sails, charts, jerry jugs, new house batteries, a kerosene or diesel heater, a second headstay, and a new 150 percent headsail. Looking through catalogs and making some phone calls will give me a good idea of the cost of each item. (I don't want to look at the total.)
- SPARE PARTS: Here's a list that grows into many small ones. Spares for rigging; engine; pumps (bilge, galley, sump, etc.); electrical system (wire, terminals, light bulbs—everything seems to take a different size); deck gear (spare shackles, line, blocks, cotter pins, deck fill key, etc.): stove, refrigeration, galley equipment; plumbing system; etc.
- REPAIR KITS: Repair kits are sold by many manufacturers for each piece of equipment they produce, and I have found them invaluable. One big advantage with a kit is knowing that every item in it is the right size, and contains replacements for just about everything that could break or wear out. As an example, we carry a repair kit for our toilet. It cost $19.25 and contains valves, washers, springs, screws, everything "expendable" ex-

cept a diaphragm. An extra diaphragm was purchased for $15.85.

- MANUALS: List every piece of gear you're taking with you. Make sure you have an operating or parts manual for each. Most vehicles with engines come with an owner's manual that explains the basics: how to start it, change the oil, bleed the fuel system and troubleshoot. It's an excellent idea to buy the larger and more detailed "shop manual." This book can cost from $15 to as much as $40, depending on the engine, and generally has to be ordered directly from the manufacturer or importer. While operating manuals are available for all electronic gear, make sure to get schematic diagrams for the wiring and circuits if they are not included. It's not likely the average layman could repair a sophisticated piece of electronics, but if you must take it to an out-of-the-way little repair shop, the work will go easier and faster if you can supply the repairman with schematics of its inner workings.
- TOOLS: If you are already accustomed to doing much of your own work, chances are you already have a good selection of tools. Give some thought to special tools that might be wanted when you're away from civilization or that might be needed in an emergency.
- PERSONAL GEAR: Don't list "everyday" items like shorts, T-shirts and underwear. List the big items that might have to be purchased or replaced before leaving, such as foul weather gear (several hundred dollars) or a new pair of boots or a good oiled-wool sweater ($60 to $100) for cold nights. Think about things that might really cause trouble if they were lost and you didn't have a replacement—prescription eyeglasses perhaps, or false teeth. Don't giggle. Dentures do get broken. Would you want to spend the second half of a trans-ocean passage gumming mashed potatoes for dinner every night?

 **Your first planning expense should be a notebook—to keep track of all the things you need to buy and do before taking off.**

- SAFETY EQUIPMENT: Unless your boat is new, it should already be equipped with the basic gear required by the Coast Guard: life jackets, flares, fog horn, etc. List the additional items that may be necessary for offshore passages, such as a life raft with survival kit, radar reflector, safety harnesses, man overboard pole, strobe light and an EPIRB (emergency position indicating radio beacon).
- MEDICAL: (See Chapter Ten for a discussion on medical preparedness.) Medical kits, as opposed to a first aid kit, can be purchased for about $50 to as much as $300, depending on their size and contents. It's a better idea to put together your own, hence the need for yet another list. Start with a list of supplies that are included with one of the larger kits and use it as a guide to what you want, and don't want. Books on emergency care usually contain suggestions for supplies, too. Discuss it with your doctor, and get prescriptions for drugs that can't be purchased over the counter. Be careful about stocking up on medicatons too far in advance, since many of them have a limited shelf life. Don't neglect a dental kit, either. They are available for $20 to $40, or get the supplies through your dentist.
- "THINGS TO DO" LIST: This is the one that can go on forever. Cross off one item, add two more. Since these lists are for "getting ready" and to get a handle on costs, don't list routine chores. "Varnish the hatch" could go on and off the list a half-dozen times during the preparation period. List the jobs that need completion before leaving. A call to my sailmaker will give me a good estimate of the cost of making an awning/rain catcher. A call to a lumber yard will tell me the cost of adding shelves in the deck house. Don't neglect domestic items. You need to visit your banker, accountant and lawyer. Get last-minute health and dental check-ups as well.
- STORES LIST: This is a fun one. It's also a list that could occupy a notebook all its own. Stores includes more than just food, it includes all those non-eatables like toothpaste, soap, toilet tissue, matches and paper towels. Much of what goes on this list will depend on where you are going and for how long. Going from New York to Florida via the Intracoastal Waterway isn't going to require the kind of stocking up (unless you choose to) that would be required for an ocean passage from New York to Europe. There's a wealth of cookbooks and cruising books that give detailed information about provisioning, but in my opinion the very best is Lin Pardey's *The Care and Feeding of the Offshore Crew*.

Making these long, detailed lists isn't something that can be done in one or two evenings. It's impossible to think of absolutely everything all at once. Start early. Six months, a year, even three or four years is not too soon. Spreading major purchases out over several years is a lot smaller jolt to the bank account than dropping $10,000 or $20,000 in a couple of weeks. But be selective about any purchases that are made a long time in advance. Some items—and electronics are a prime example—are actually decreasing in price. It might be better to put the money where it will earn interest, and make a note to yourself that it is earmarked for something specific.

 **Start planning early. This way you can pay for big expenses over a longer period of time.**

If the lists start looking horrendous, try rearranging some of them according to priorities. The equipment list is especially prone to getting out of hand. Try to be realistic (are radar, loran, sat nav and weather facsimile *really* necessary to get away from the dock?) and put each item into one of three categories:

- No doubt about it, gotta have it.
- Can put it off, maybe for a long time.
- When I get rich.

The same can be done for a must-do list. The categories are: do it now, procrastinate and who cares?

Doubling is a great way to spread out the cost of provisioning. Start buying extras of non-perishable items on every trip to the supermarket. Instead of buying one tube of toothpaste or bottle of shampoo, double up and buy two, or even three, especially if something is on sale. The few extra dollars will scarcely be noticed. But do that for six months or a year, and it will be noticed when the major provisioning expenditures start. Even for those who won't be stocking up for a passage, it can still make a difference. Stock up while you still have a job and it will help ease the transition to living on less income when you quit or retire.

The Cost of Escaping

At least six months, more preferably a year before leaving, start keeping a detailed record of all expenses. The only way to do this accurately is to write it down at the end of *every* day. Unless you are planning an escape by sea and already are living aboard, land costs will be reflected (rent or house payments, utilities, car, etc.). But it will provide a good handle on what you now spend for food, entertainment, medical care, etc. While many big expenses will be eliminated, other smaller ones will be added. For instance, your house may have a washer and dryer, but laundry will become a weekly expense unless you choose Grandma's washboard routine.

The expense of owning a car will be replaced by the cost of public

TABLE 1	**AVERAGE MONTHLY CRUISING COSTS OF FOUR**		
	$6,000/year		**$7,200/year**
Category	**Monthly Average**	**Monthly %**	**Monthly Average**
Stores	$200	40%	$200
Boat expense	70	14	72
Entertainment	115	23	102
Dockage	15	3	18
Fuel and oil	25	5	30
Clothing	5	1	6
Transportation	5	1	6
Medical	5	1	6
Ice	13	2½	12
Stove fuel	5	1	3
Laundry	10	2	9
Telephone calls	5	1	6
Mail	12	2½	12
Insurance	0	0	100
Miscellaneous	15	3	18
Totals	$500	100%	$600

transportation, car rentals and/or the one-time cost of buying a bicycle. For just about everybody, the cost of postage goes up. Cruising people tend to write more letters than they did when they lived ashore, and usually pick up the cost of mail forwarding. One cost that generally decreases for voyaging sailors is medical expenses. Cruisers become more self-sufficient and less prone to run to a doctor for every little ache and pain. And for everyone away from the stress of city life, there are fewer aches and pains and headaches, anyway.

Table 1 shows how four different couples might budget their incomes. The numbers are based on averages arrived at by comparing real expenses of a number of different cruising people, myself included. Some costs remained fairly consistent regardless of income— food, clothing, medical expenses and laundry. Other costs, like entertainment, went up along with spendable income. People with higher incomes, as a rule, went dockside more often and were more likely to carry insurance. Few people I spoke with used a home-base manager other than an unpaid family member, but the majority of them used a mail-forwarding service.

"TYPICAL" COUPLES

$7,200/year	$9,600/year		$12,000/year	
Monthly %	Monthly Average	Monthly %	Monthly Average	Monthly %
33%	$240	30%	$ 240	24%
12	96	12	120	12
17	128	16	150	15
3	100	12½	200	20
5	32	4	30	3
1	8	1	10	1
1	8	1	10	1
1	8	1	7	½
2	12	1½	0	0
½	8	1	3	½
1½	12	1½	10	1
1	8	1	20	2
2	16	2	20	2
17	100	12½	150	15
3	24	3	30	3
100%	$800	100%	$1,000	100%

To make it easier to compare costs and plug in your own figures, I divided yearly costs into a monthly average, even though several items reflect a few large expenses rather than a monthly outlay. Boat expense includes a yearly haul-out that means a major expenditure for just one month. The stores column often means a few major provisionings during the year with small amounts being spent week to week. A few notes are in order about some of the categories:

- STORES: This includes food and all items normally purchased at the same time—shampoo, paper towels, cigarettes, cat food, etc.
- VEHICLE EXPENSE: Includes equipment purchases, haul-out, maintenance—varnish, paint, etc.
- ENTERTAINMENT: Eating out, movies, liquor, etc.
- FUEL AND OIL: Includes main engine and outboard.
- TRANSPORTATION: Bus, train, car rental, etc.
- MEDICAL: Doctor, dentist, prescriptions.
- MAIL: Includes cost of forwarding service.
- INSURANCE: Boat, health, and/or life.

When making estimates of your projected expenses, based on what you are spending now and by looking at Table 1, don't try to be too Spartan—unless it really does reflect your existing lifestyle. It is foolish to give up a simple pleasure like wine with the evening meal if it is something you have enjoyed for years, just for the sake of saving a few dollars each month in the food or entertainment category. Shop around for a less expensive wine, perhaps, but don't give it up altogether. Cruising, or any form of escape, is supposed to be fun, not an exercise in masochism.

Don't plan on drastically reducing the food budget by fishing and foraging, either. It just doesn't happen. Now don't get me wrong, many people do fish and do it very well. And I've been in places where avocados were free for the picking and berries could be gathered along the paths. But it's not something to be counted on. Plan on your food budget being close to what it is now and look at fishing as a nice bonus.

 **Don't give up simple pleasures—
like wine with meals—just to save a
few dollars. Your escape is nothing
if it's not fun.**

Money can be saved by anchoring or camping out. But here again, don't plan on eliminating the expense altogether. Everyone likes to stay someplace nice once in awhile—to do work requiring lots of electricity, to take advantage of shower facilities—or just for the fun of being close to the action. Sailors will find it nice—even a necessity —to be able to step from dock to boat when provisioning for a long passage and transferring hundreds of pounds of gear and groceries.

There are always ways to cut back. For example, the cruising costs shown in Table 1 include a yearly haul-out. This is always a major expense, but one that can be avoided by careening the boat (putting it over on its side in a tidal zone) to clean and paint the bottom. That's assuming you're in an area where careening is possible. The cost of bottom paint, of course, still will have to be included. Often the job can be put off for two years or longer by diving and cleaning the bottom in the water. Every cruiser I know who has scuba gear swears it is one of the best investments they ever made. People with campers and RVs, of course, will do well to learn how to change their oil and do regular tune-ups.

Supplementing Your Income

Picking up work along the way sometimes is feasible, but for most people it should not be counted on as a way of completely financing an escape. There are exceptions of course. Careers like sailmaker, writer, mechanic, photographer, chef, waiter or waitress are all portable skills. But setting out virtually penniless and hoping to find work in every port or city is best left to the young and daring.

 **You can catch fish and pick berries. But part of the art of escape is being realistic. Plan on your food budget being close to what it is now.**

Many do, however, take "work breaks" of six months or a year, but they don't wait until they are flat broke before they start job hunting. The art of escape is to set out with enough money to live comfortably for a certain period of time, and planning the trip to temporarily end wherever you are reasonably sure of finding work. More often than not, this means going back to the United States, or to a U.S. territory. Many countries—including the U.S.—have strict laws about granting work permits to foreigners.

It seems, however, that those who decide to stop and work *always* seem to find it, and one of the biggest reasons is a willingness to accept any kind of job that's available. Several years ago my friends Ed LaVigueur and June MacQuarrie quit their jobs in electronics, moved aboard their boat *Impulse* and left New York for a leisurely cruise down the waterway to Florida. *Impulse* wasn't paid off yet, but they had saved enough money to make payments, go on the cruise and have a cushion to fall back on while they looked for work. Within two weeks of arriving in Florida they both had landed good-paying jobs in the electronics field. Of course, it helped that they had training in a field that—then at least—was short-handed.

After paying off the loan on *Impulse* and rebuilding the cruising fund, Ed and June headed out to visit the rest of Florida and the Bahamas. The next work break was in the Florida Keys, where Ed went to work at a cement plant and June made shell jewelry for a gift shop and worked part-time cleaning rooms at a local motel. A far cry from electronics, but it kept them going.

"We were ready for more adventuresome cruising," said June, "we wanted to see the Caribbean." That meant another year back in Melbourne and the better-paying electronics jobs, to fund a Caribbean cruise and equip *Impulse* for offshore work.

They fell in love with the Caribbean, the warm sun, the crystal-clear water, the fantastic sailing. When it was time to go back to work, neither wanted to leave. They heard jobs were available in St. Thomas, U.S. Virgin Islands. Did they find work there? You bet they did—Ed as a diesel mechanic and June keeping books for a nursery and landscaping company. It gave them two full years of Caribbean cruising.

April of 1983 found them back in Florida for a major refitting of *Impulse* and yet another work break at their old careers to pay for more adventures.

Ed and June's story is just one of many. It happens over and over. People save enough to take off for a year or two, planning a return to their old jobs and old lifestyles at the end of that time. But they discover their escapes suit them so well they will do anything to keep going. And they do: they go to work, at anything and everything.

 **You can supplement your escape "kitty" by working as you go. But, unless you have special— marketable—skills, you'll have to be willing to take whatever job comes along.**

Back in 1975 I went east to pick up a schooner. The plan was to cruise for a year while bringing the boat back to California, then return to my old job as a naval architect. Almost seven years later I was still east, living aboard, cruising and deep into a new career as a writer. I finally did return to California, but not to go back to the old lifestyle. No, I'm hooked and will keep working until I can afford to head out again for distant waters. It's been done so many times before, and by so many others. It takes planning and saving, but taking off for that escape of a lifetime is within the reach of anyone who makes up their mind they are going to do it.

CHAPTER FOUR

Escaping with the Kids

The Artful Getaway is Educational, Too

Whether or not you should take along your children on a lengthy escape is a question roundly debated by child psychologists, school administrators, judges and parents. I'm most inclined to listen to parents and their children.

Since 1979 Tom and Jean Shaffer and their two sons have been living and cruising aboard their schooner *Gitana*. Jean, a former schoolteacher, has strong opinions about maintaining the quality of her children's education while cruising. The youngest son completed seventh and eighth grades through Calvert correspondence school and all four years of high school through the University of Nebraska's Divison of Continuing Studies, a correspondence school for high school-level students. Their oldest boy finished his last two years of high school with the University of Nebraska program.

"We, as parents, and they, as students, found it rewarding. Cruising, especially if it brings one into contact with new cultures, is an education in the finest sense of the word. It teaches a child things he would not learn in school," Jean says.

Both Tom and Jean believe they have given their sons the best of both worlds, the experience of cruising and an education that has prepared them well for college and beyond.

I had the pleasure of meeting the Shaffers and their youngest son recently in Florida. Mike, a very personable teen-ager, had taken a summer job at a boatyard. He didn't seem at all maladjusted by his lack of a normal high school education. Quite the contrary. He was friendly and outgoing, had quickly made many friends and readily accepted responsibilities at the yard.

That same year in Florida I also met a lively, frecklefaced redheaded bundle of energy named Zorana Jordan. She was 12 years old and had been living aboard and cruising with her parents and a dog named French for three years. A student with Calvert School, Zorana spent from four to six hours a day working on her lessons. She told me she didn't think kids on shore were stupid, exactly, but she did believe that Calvert students learned more than those in public schools. Zorana did admit that she sometimes missed "having 28 or 30 kids around all the time" and visiting easily with her friends. But

34

she was quick to add that she thought it was only a "small disadvantage" and she bubbled with enthusiasm when she talked about the advantages of cruising.

"I like to sail. I like to travel. I like being able to swim so much and to row my dinghy. Mostly I like all the interesting people I get to meet."

But later she confided that she was not at all sure she wanted to go through high school entirely in correspondence courses. She thought she might want to "live in a *place*, and go to dances and fun things like that." High school was still several years away, but already she was thinking about what it would mean and what she might be giving up.

I remember, too, when Sy and Vicki Carkhuff moved ashore so their son could play ball and attend school with his peers—but only after they had sailed around the world. Vicki missed cruising, and longed for the day when they would go again. But she felt it was not fair to any of them to continue when it meant so much to David to lead a shore life until he finished school.

I think it's easier to decide to take off with young children. Once teen-agers and well on their way to adulthood, the wishes of older children must be considered equally with the rest of the crew. Teen-agers are no different than adults in one respect: some of them will love the escape and some won't. Your escape is not going to be wonderful with someone aboard who is unhappy or resentful.

What are the alternatives, if a son or daughter doesn't want to go? One way is simply to wait until your children are through school and have left home. In our case, Taz's 17-year-old son lives with us. He has only one year of high school left. He may decide to cruise with us later on, but it is very important to him to finish high school and graduate with his friends. We live aboard dockside, and see it as an extra year to get *Alliance* equipped the way we want her—in addition to another year in which to build the cruising kitty.

Another alternative, although an expensive one, is a private boarding school. The cost for this can vary greatly. Or a relative or close family friend may be willing to act as guardian while you're away. When you add up the cost of tuition, clothing, transportation, room and board and spending money, it could easily equal the cost of your escape. And you'll want your youngsters to be with you for holidays and vacations, so figure in round-trip airfares several times a year. It's no wonder most parents, other than the very wealthy, opt either for correspondence courses or for staying put until the kids are out of school.

While most cruising parents do use correspondence schools, it is possible to instruct your own children. But exercise this option only if you are qualified. Joanne Sandstrom, a high school teacher by profession, cruised for five years with her husband and their two teenage sons. Rather than use correspondence courses, Sandstrom handled the boys' education herself. She brought along textbooks and an extensive reference library. Her oldest son did well enough on his high school equivalency test and college entrance exams to be accepted by the University of California at Berkeley, San Diego State *and* Princeton. Her youngest son is now a senior in public school and on the honor roll.

Let's take a closer look at some of the correspondence schools.

Calvert School
105 Tuscany Road
Baltimore, Maryland 21210

As far as I know, Calvert School is the only correspondence school for elementary-level children. It covers kindergarten through the eighth grade. While cruising, I have met dozens of people using Calvert. I hear nothing but praise from parents *and* their offspring.

Some noteworthy sailors are former Calvert students, including Warwick Tompkins. In 1932, at the tender age of two weeks, Tompkins (and his parents) took off aboard the 85-foot German pilot schooner *Wanderbird*. They made numerous Atlantic crossings and sailed around Cape Horn on their way to San Francisco. Both Warwick and his sister were enrolled in Calvert School. In a letter to the west coast publication *Latitude 38,* Tompkins writes that when he finally entered public school in 1941 he was able to "coast" for four years because his education through Calvert had been so thorough. He adds that he found the public school courses "unimaginative and dull."

The home instruction courses are modeled after the curriculum of the Calvert Day School, which operates as an independent school. Course revisions are made after evaluation and testing in the day school, which serves as a kind of laboratory for the correspondence courses.

Founded in 1897, Calvert School is a member of the Educational Records Bureau, and its courses are approved by Maryland's department of education.

 **Taking off is easier with young children. You must respect the feelings of older children, who may have their own opinions about your impending escape. The best planning won't make your escape enjoyable if it is shared with someone who is resentful and unhappy.**

The courses are designed to be administered by parents with no teaching experience. A manual is provided with each course that gives day-to-day and step-by-step instructions. Equally important, the school offers an advisory teaching service for grades one through eight (not available for the kindergarten course). A Calvert teacher is assigned to each student to grade papers, make comments on the child's work and offer advice and encouragement to the parent/teacher.

Although the advisory teaching service is an option, it doesn't make much sense *not* to use it. Without the service, Calvert cannot furnish transcripts of grades to the schools or testify that a course has been completed and passed.

Virtually all materials are supplied with each course: lesson plans, books, paper, even pencils, ruler and crayons.

Among the subjects covered through Calvert courses are reading, spelling, language usage, composition, arithmetic, history, science and geography, along with "enrichment" subjects such as art history, mythology and poetry. The course for each grade level is designed for a normal school year of about nine months. The school suggests three-and-a-half to five hours of study each day. Students can, however, proceed at their own pace. Jean Shaffer reports Mike completed both seventh and eighth grade in one normal school year.

Tuition fees for each course are shown in Table 1. The fee for the advisory teaching service includes return of test papers and the teacher's letters by air mail to addresses outside the continental United States.

Shipping charges for a complete course (which weighs, on the average, 20–22 pounds) are included in the tuition. Shipment is by parcel post in the United States and regular surface mail to foreign countries. Calvert estimates four to six weeks for overseas delivery. That could be a long time to stay in one port waiting for lessons to arrive, so Calvert will ship by air mail or air freight but you must pay the postage. The school requires clients to estimate the charges to their location and include the amount with each order. The school will refund any excess.

TABLE 1   **TUITION FOR CALVERT SCHOOL**

Costs shown are for *each* grade. They include tuition fee, lesson manual, textbooks, workbooks, supplies for the school year and shipment by book rate or parcel post in the United States and by regular surface mail to foreign addresses.

Prices as of January 1983.

Course	Cost
Kindergarten Course	$135.00
Grades 1 through 4	$235.00
Advisory Teaching Service, Grades 1-4	$120.00
	$355.00
Grades 5 and 6	$255.00
Advisory Teaching Service, Grades 5-6	$120.00
	$375.00
Grades 7 and 8	$255.00
Advisory Teaching Service, Grades 7-8	$130.00
	$385.00

University of Nebraska, Lincoln
Division of Continuing Studies
269 Nebraska Center for Continuing Education
Lincoln, Nebraska 68583

University of Nebraska's Division of Continuing Studies is one of several institutions offering a high school correspondence program. Founded in 1929 and accredited by the North Central Association of Colleges and Schools and the Nebraska State Department of Education, the school had an enrollment of 1,500 students in 1982 that included children of diplomats and missionaries as well as cruising people.

The school requires each student's work to be supervised by an adult approved by the school administration. The supervisor must be someone other than a parent or relative, but the school *will* grant permission under unusual circumstances. Obviously a small boat at sea is an unusual circumstance, unless another crewmember can serve as tutor. But parents must make special application to act as their own child's supervisor.

The Nebraska program offers more than 130 courses covering grades nine through 12. Each course covers one semester's work (18 weeks). To earn a diploma, a student must earn 180 credit hours, of which at least 20 credit hours must be earned through the Nebraska program regardless of the number of transer credits the student had upon enrollment.

The required courses for graduation, totaling 90 credit hours, are:

- Three years of English
- Two years of science
- Two years of math
- Two years of social studies, including one year of American history, one semester of American government and a one-semester elective.

This leaves 90 credit hours as electives, although—just as a student on shore—anyone planning to go on to college should investigate the entrance requirements at the colleges or universities they would like to attend.

The elective courses appear comparable with those offered by most large high schools. They include art, languages, industrial and business education, home economics and agriculture.

Tuition is paid for each course on enrollment. All materials are provided, including textbooks, kits, even a ream of paper for the typing class. To get an idea of the typical cost for a high school semester, I asked Taz's son to go through the list of courses and pick out the same ones he was taking in public school. The results are shown in Table 2. These courses are for his first semester, junior year (grade 11). The second semester could be a little less, since some of the full year (two semester) courses use the same textbook for both semesters.

His general science course could prove interesting for all the crew, since it includes kits for chemical experiments, complete with alcohol burners, glass beakers and flasks. I think I'd want to be dockside or anchored in calm waters before any experimenting took place!

I chose air mail postage for the example. The charge for surface shipment within the continental United States is $7 for each course. For mailing to foreign ports, the school recommends air freight, insured and/or registered shipment. To do this, they request an initial $7 per course, and will send a bill for the postage balance.

The Nebraska school program includes a counseling service for its high school students, so your child can receive professional guidance in choosing courses and mapping out a study program.

American School
850 East 58th Street
Chicago, Illinois 60637

American School was founded in Boston, Massachusetts, in 1897, and moved to Chicago in 1902. It is accredited by the North Central Association of Colleges and Schools and by the Accrediting Commission of the National Home Study Council. Enrollment is approximately 40,000 students.

The school has conducted a series of studies over the past 25 years to determine the success rate of its graduates who go on to college. The latest study (Table 3) is based upon reports from college registrars at 808 colleges and universities and covers enrollment of 1,361

TABLE 2 **FEES FOR ONE SEMESTER, ELEVENTH GRADE COURSE, UNIVERSITY OF NEBRASKA'S DIVISION OF CONTINUING STUDIES**

Prices as of September, 1982.

Course	Cost
General Business (5 hours—½ unit)	
Tuition	$44.00
Textbook, *General Business for Everyday Living*	5.94
Syllabus, *General Business*	9.75
Handling fees, airmail postage	10.50
	$ 70.19
Eleventh Grade English (5 hours—½ unit)	
Tuition	$44.00
Textbook, *The New Building Better English*	4.70
Textbook, *Adventures in American Literature*	18.19
Syllabus, *Eleventh Grade English*	10.00
Handling fees, airmail postage	10.50
	$ 87.39
Automotive Mechanics (5 hours—½ unit)	
Tuition	$44.00
Textbook, *The Auto Book*	19.11
Syllabus, *Automotive Mechanics*	11.40
Handling fees, airmail postage	10.50
	$ 85.01
American History (5 hours—½ unit)	
Tuition	$44.00
Textbook, *Rise of the American Nation*	15.56
Syllabus, *American History*	10.25
Handling fees, airmail postage	10.50
	$ 80.31
General Science (5 hours—½ unit)	
Tuition	$44.00
Textbook, *Modern Physical Science*	9.52
Syllabus, *General Science*	12.35
Experiment Kit 3SAK-1	16.95
Experiment Kit 3SAK-2	6.45
Experiment Kit 3SCK	6.46
Handling fees, airmail postage	10.50
	$106.23
Total	$429.13

American School graduates. The results provide a good argument against those who claim that correspondence schools don't provide a good education. Note that in each rating category, American School graduates supassed the performance of other college students, most of whom, it must be assumed, were blessed with a more formal education.

Unlike the University of Nebraska correspondence program, American School does not require an approved supervisor. It does, however, require that local principals authorize the enrollment by signing the enrollment application form. This is something to keep in mind when starting a cruise or an escape during the summer months.

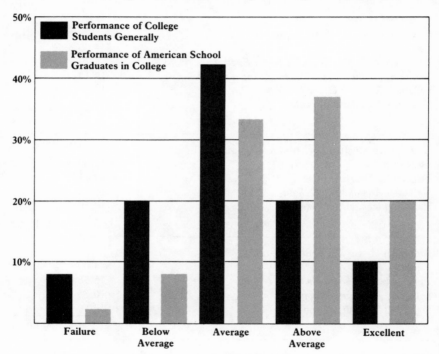

TABLE 3   **COLLEGE PROFILE OF AMERICAN SCHOOL GRADUATES**

The achievement of American School graduates (gray), as rated by their college registrars, compared with that of college students generally (black). The study is based upon reports from college registrars at 808 colleges and universities and covers enrollment of 1,361 American School graduates.

Chart courtesy of American School, Chicago, Illinois.

Get the principal's signature *before* leaving home port for the far horizon.

American School offers about 100 courses. It requires 16 units for graduation (compared with 18 units required by Nebraska), but students don't have as much flexibility in selecting courses. Two programs are offered, one for students planning on entering college and another for those interested only in a high school diploma.

 It is possible to teach your own children. But it's not a reasonable option unless you're absolutely qualified.

Required subjects for the college preparatory high school course are:

- Algebra I (1 unit)
- Biology (1 unit)
- Planning Your Career (1 unit)
- Civics, Social (Government) (1 unit)
- Understanding English 1 (1 unit)
- Understanding English 2 (1 unit)
- Geometry (1 unit)
- United States History (1 unit)
- American Literature (1 unit)
- English Literature (1 unit)
- Essential Mathematics 1 (1 unit)
- Essential Mathematics 2 (1 unit)
- Psychology (1 unit)

The remaining three units are electives.
Required subjects for the general high school course are:

- Planning Your Career (1 unit)
- Civics, Social (Government) (1 unit)
- Practical English (1 unit)
- Understanding English 1 (½ unit)

- United States History (1 unit)
- World Literature (1 unit)
- Essential Mathematics 1 (1 unit)
- Essential Mathematics 2 (1 unit)
- Psychology (1 unit)
- General Science (1 unit)
- Speech—How to Talk More Effectively (½ unit)

Electives round out the remaining six units.

Elective subjects offered include English, science, industrial arts, math, languages (French and Spanish), social studies, business, art and home economics.

Cost for the American School appears to be almost half that of Nebraska's Division of Continuing Studies. I don't know why this is so, although it might be because it has almost four times the number of students. For comparison, I calculated courses similar to the ones young Taz picked out for the Nebraska school (see Table 4). The cost for each class is based on one unit, or a full year (two semesters). The courses can be taken as half-units, or single semesters, but this adds an additional $10 to each course. By enrolling for a full year, instead of one semester at a time, you save $100 a year. The matriculation fee of $12 is only paid once—the first time a student enrolls. All textbooks, study guides and other materials are included in the course price.

American School students are eligible for scholarships. Winners are selected from the highest ranking graduates for each calendar year. These awards now include a $2,000 scholarship, one for $1,000 and 20 scholarships of $400 each. All awards are paid as tuition to the college or university selected by its winner.

While these two schools are probably the best known and most widely used high school correspondence programs, there are others. Many large universities offer correspondence curriculum for high school students. In California, the University of California at Berkeley offers such a program. Your best bet is to call any college or university in your area, or contact your state university.

Also, a publication is available—*The Independent Study Catalog*—that lists high school, college and graduate-level correspondence courses offered by the 72 colleges and universities that are members of the Independent Study Division of the National University Contin-

TABLE 4 **FEES FOR ONE SEMESTER, AND A FULL YEAR, ELEVENTH GRADE COURSE, AMERICAN SCHOOL**

All textbooks, study guides and other materials are included in the price of each course. Prices as of March 1983.

Course	Cost
SINGLE TERM	
General Business (½ unit)	$ 47.00
American Literature (½ unit)	50.00
Automotive Engines (½ unit)	55.00
United States History (½ unit)	44.00
General Science (½ unit)	42.00
Matriculation Fee (one time only)	12.00
	$250.00

This is for one semester; it costs less to enroll for the year. A semester price is one-half the yearly fee, plus $10 per course. For a year (two semesters) the cost would be:

Course	Cost
FULL YEAR	
General Business (1 unit)	$ 74.00
American Literature (1 unit)	80.00
Automotive Engines (1 unit)	90.00
United States History (1 unit)	68.00
General Science (1 unit)	64.00
Matriculation Fee (one time only)	12.00
	$388.00

Enrolling for a full year results in a savings of $100.00.

uing Education Association (NUCEA). The catalog can be ordered for $4.50 from:

National University Continuing Education Association
Suite 360
One Dupont Circle
Washington, D.C. 20036

College-Level Correspondence Courses

Many correspondence programs offer college-level courses, allowing high school students as well as graduates to enroll. However, the number of correspondence-school credit hours that you can apply toward a college degree varies with each institution. The University of Nebraska, for example, allows between 25 and 60 semester hours to apply towards a bachelor's degree, depending on the student's course of study.

Tuition for college credit courses is $36 a credit hour. As an example, a freshman English course in composition and literature, at three credit hours for the first semester, costs $108 for tuition, $11 for the syllabus and $22.76 for text and required reading, for a total cost of $141.76 plus postage.

While the school does not require a supervisor for college courses, it does require examinations to be taken in the presence of an approved proctor. There are usually two exams for each course, a midterm and a final. This could be an inconvenience, since the proctor cannot be a parent. Before an exam is mailed to the proctor a completed "Request for Examination" form must be sent to, and approved by, the school. After locating a proctor, plan on staying in one place during the exam process. Approved proctors could be high school or college teachers or administrators or, in a foreign country, U.S. embassy or consular officials.

Numerous other colleges and universities offer some of their courses by correspondence. As mentioned earlier, *The Independent Study Catalog* is a good reference guide for college-level as well as high school courses.

College Entrance Exams

Most colleges require that applicants pass either the American College Test (ACT) or the Scholastic Aptitude Test (SAT). Contact the colleges or universities to which your child is applying to find out which test they prefer. To find out when and where the tests will be given, check at any U.S. high school or write directly to the testing organizations:

(ACT) The American College Testing Program
Mrs. Billie Norris, Correspondent
Test Administration and Security
P.O. Box 168
Iowa City, IA 52240

(SAT) College Entrance Examination Board
College Board Admissions, Testing Program
Box 592
Princeton, NJ 08540

If You're Divorced

This is not a pleasant subject, but if you are a divorced parent with custody of your children and are about to take them with you on your escape, take heed.

In 1980, after spending six years building their dream boat, a woman and her husband were about to leave Northern California for a lengthy cruise to Mexico and the South Pacific, taking along her three children by a former marriage. All the children were enrolled in Calvert School. Just before leaving, her ex-husband sued for a change of custody. She retained custody, but only as long as she remained in California. The courts allowed them to move as far as San Diego, but would not let them take the children out of the country.

In 1981, they decided to sail to Mexico for awhile, despite the court order. Her ex-husband was not happy about it, but they agreed verbally to a visitation schedule. Shortly afterwards she was again sued for change of custody. When she returned for the court appearance she discovered she was also charged with child theft and spent a week in jail because she couldn't post bail. The woman finally lost custody of her children, the court ruling that the father lived in a "home" in a "normal" neighborhood. The woman and her husband still live aboard, but are now working to pay off her legal fees instead of adding to their escape fund.

This is not an isolated case. Another woman lost custody of her two young children because she wanted to take them cruising. Her ex-husband agreed to keep the kids while she and her new husband sailed from Mexico to Tahiti. He had agreed to allow the children to join them there. (Again, the children were enrolled in Calvert School.) But on arriving in Tahiti, she found that her ex-husband had gone to court and had been awarded temporary custody on the grounds the children needed a "more stable environment." At this writing, the woman is back in the United States fighting to get her children returned. The boat is on its way back from Tahiti. The cruise is over.

 **If you're divorced and have custody of your children, make sure to consult with an attorney before taking them with you on an extended escape.**

Certainly an ex-spouse has every right to expect reasonable visitation privileges. That may prove extremely difficult—both from the standpoint of money and time—if one parent is in the States and the other in Europe or the South Pacific. However, even if a visitation schedule is worked out, the courts still can rule you are not providing a suitable environment or a good education for your children, forcing you to choose between losing them or giving up your grand escape plans.

No easy answers exist. Once the matter goes to court, it appears to be a no-win situation for everyone. Legal expenses alone can end a cruise or dream escape. The lesson is that all custody issues should be discussed with an attorney before taking off. It's going to be a long time before those in our judicial system see the advantages cruising and other forms of escape offer youngsters—the possibility of an excellent formal education, the incredible informal education that travel provides and the lessons in self-reliance and self-discipline that are such an integral part of sailing and living on a small boat.

CHAPTER FIVE

Tending the Home Fires

Do you really trust Uncle Harry?

Sailing off into the sunset, free as a bird, with no worries and no problems back home is an appealing prospect. In reality, of course, it is just about impossible to take off and never give a single thought to what is left behind.

I do know two sailors who did it: one owned the IRS a bundle and the other, too, was on the lam. The rest of us, who want to stay in touch *and* keep the IRS from getting on our backs, may need someone on the home front looking after our interests. Some of the things a home-base manager can do for you are:

- Pay bills and insurance premiums on time
- Make deposits and reconcile bank statements
- Collect rents and other monies due
- Manage real estate
- Receive and forward mail
- Provide a telephone number for credit card calls
- Handle the investment portfolio
- Transfer money on request or at specified intervals
- Locate you in an emergency
- Prepare tax forms

There really are two kinds of home-base managers, the kind who pays bills and handles other routine chores, and the type who handles major investments for high-income clients, who acts in your place in important matters.

For Whom the Manager Toils

Anyone with substantial business holdings or investments, a large portfolio of stocks and bonds, numerous bank transactions or monthly bills to pay, or matters requiring legal services, will undoubtedly find a home-base manager a great help, if not a necessity. That assumes, however, they have enough confidence in the manager to sail away, leaving their affairs entirely in his hands.

50

Some cruisers find it is just too much trouble, too costly, or too difficult to handle even a relatively few business transactions by long distance. The mail is slow; they worry whether a check sent from a remote island will make it all the way to a Chicago-based insurance company. Or, it just takes too many weeks before they know for sure that an expected rent check really got deposited in the bank account per the pre-arranged schedule. Their escape is more relaxed and more enjoyable when they know someone is back home, close to the action and able to handle just about any problem that might crop up— someone who will *call* the tenant if the rent check is late, or transfer funds from savings to checking when the account gets low.

 **In reality, it is almost impossible to take off and never think about what you've left behind. A home-base manager is one way to sail off into the sunset and still make sure the bills are paid.**

Ann and Tom Selck, on their 10-month cruise to the U.S. Virgin Islands, deducted as much as possible automatically from their checking account, and paid the rest of the bills themselves. Even still, Ann says, on their next cruise she will arrange to have someone at home, either a relative or their accountant, to take care of their bill-paying.

Not everyone finds it necessary to hire one individual. With good relationships already established with a banker, an accountant, an attorney, a stockbroker and whomever else, it may be important to maintain these relationships, particularly if eventually you plan on returning to the old lifestyle. But maintaining long-distance correspondence with all of them could turn out to be a balancing act that just isn't worth all the trouble.

Think about how often you call these people now, how pressing the problems really are. Consider what would happen if you *didn't* call. Would the world fall apart? Would it mean financial ruin? Or are you just confirming decisions they are capable of making on their own, anyway? Obviously, talk to them all before leaving. What suggestions can they offer about the best way to handle things in your absence? You may well find it's easiest after all to delegate one as the manager, to give him or her the responsibility of keeping tabs on the others. It would give you one source to contact on a regular basis, one person to rely on to keep everything running smoothly and in your best interests. It should be someone capable of making decisions, and knowledgeable enough to know when the only right decision is to contact you. Deciding on the right person for *this* job isn't always easy.

Choosing a Manager

Trust doesn't develop overnight, in a few afternoons of interviews or even on the recommendation of a close friend. Trust is earned over a long period of time. I'm sure that's the biggest reason why so many cruising people choose family members to handle their affairs. And it's usually someone in their immediate family—a parent, or a son or daughter. Wayne Carpenter reports his arrangements with a brother-in-law were less than satisfactory, but everyone else I spoke with (who were using a parent or offspring) were completely happy with the way things worked.

Anyone escaping who, for whatever reason, is unable to use a relative, faces more of a challenge in finding a manager. Regardless of the profession (bankers, stockbrokers, etc.) it inevitably turns out to be someone with whom they also have developed a friendship, and someone with whom they have worked for several years at a minimum.

It works both ways. Every potential home-base manager I interviewed was willing to handle business and personal affairs for a client, but *only* for a client they have known for a long time. No one was willing to take on a responsibility for somebody "walking in off the street." Most said they would insist on a legal agreement, spelling out precisely what they would be expected to do, both for the client's protection as well as their own. Additionally, they would expect the client to telephone them periodically, and keep them informed as to their whereabouts as much as possible.

Before choosing a home-base manager, think about those people already helping you manage your affairs. If you weren't on the scene, would it mean financial ruination?

Interestingly, only two accountants and no one else would give me a quote, or even a rough estimate, of what they would charge. "Too many variables," they said, or "We'd have to try it for a few months and figure out what was *really* involved."

I gave two accountants the following list and asked what they would charge to perform these services.

- Receive and hold my mail, then forward it twice a month.
- Receive two or three checks a month and deposit them at once using bank-by-mail envelopes I would provide.
- Reconcile my monthly bank statement.
- Pay bills, perhaps three or four a month.
- Allow me to use her phone number for credit card calls, then bill me or withdraw the amount from my checking account.
- Compute annual taxes and mail estimated income taxes quarterly.
- Transfer money about once a month on receiving instructions from me either by mail or telephone.
- Send me an itemized monthly statement of all transactions.

My own accountant, Joan Curtis, said she would do it all, except for income taxes, for $100 a month. The taxes would have to be billed separately. She would require a written agreement between us, and a limited power of attorney.

The other accountant, Jim Sprague, quoted $200-$250 for all the services. He said he would base his fee on the time involved, but also on the huge responsibility he would be assuming.

For those with fairly uncomplicated dealings, several options are available. Investment decisions such as trading stocks and bonds are complicated. But not such activities as cashing in and reinvesting certificates of deposit on prearranged instructions, or receiving dividend checks and placing them in a money market fund.

An accountant is a good choice for a home-base manager. He or she is already familiar with your financial condition, as mine is, and thus is in a better position to assume more responsibility for bills and bank deposits. Accountants are typically thorough and conscientious, not likely to forget a payment or misplace a stack of mail.

An attorney is another good choice. He or she would undoubtedly have a secretary handle most of the bookkeeping chores, but presumably would monitor everything closely. Depending on the type of attorney, he can handle more complicated investment holdings than can an accountant. Sy and Vicki Carkhuff, who were both stockbrokers before leaving on their round-the-world cruise, lived off stock market income for most of their five-year trip (1973–1978). They granted full power of attorney, not to a stockbroker, but to a friend who is a tax and trust attorney. Sy told me he had so much faith in his manager he only contacted him twice in the entire five years.

 **Inevitably, whoever you finally choose as your home-base manager turns out to be someone who also is a trusted friend.**

Another possibility for someone with few financial dealings might be a secretarial service. But approach this arrangement with caution. Work with the service for at least a couple of months before leaving to make sure all instructions are being interpreted correctly. I know one sailor who used a secretarial service to handle his mail and his child support payments. He opened a separate bank account just for child support, then wrote out a year's worth of checks, signed and pre-dated. On the appropriate day each month, the service mailed a check to his ex-wife. He could have made similar arrangements with a bank. I would have felt safer asking my bank to perform this service than leaving a stack of signed checks with a secretarial service.

Bankers and stockbrokers are useful in their respective fields, but I don't think either is a likely candidate as an all-around manager. A banker can help set up a program for automatic payments and money transfers, but is not going to offer his phone number so you have a telephone credit card. While a broker will offer advice on investments, it's doubtful he'll have much interest in bookkeeping chores or sorting through your mail.

Gainor Roberts and George Cranston, who spent several years living aboard and cruising the east coast of the United States, made extensive use of both their banker and stockbroker. Gainor had banked at the same small Rhode Island bank for years, and knew the bank manager and several of the officers quite well. So they were willing to provide a number of bookkeeping services not normally available.

 **Trust works both ways. Nobody would want to take on the responsibilities of a home-base manager who isn't familiar with your personal affairs.**

George and Gainor had a large portfolio of stocks and bonds, and were able to live off the dividends and interest without dipping into the initial investment. Their broker had "stock power," a form signed by either George or Gainor for *each* stock certificate, giving the broker power to buy or sell any security in their absence. Even though Gainor contacted him by phone every three months just to see how everything was going, she gave him free reign to trade as he chose. Gainor is quick to point out, however, that he had been a personal friend for many years, and that she worked closely with him for three years before going cruising and before she granted him stock power.

And look at it from the other side. Unless a broker knows his client extremely well, he is not likely to even want such discretionary power. Most will recommend an investment counselor, instead. Brokers only make money when they buy or sell a security, and the possibility exists for a conflict of interest. While a conscientious broker realizes that unless transactions are in the client's best interest he won't retain that client for very long, an out-of-touch cruising client could lose a lot of money before he realized what was happening.

An investment counselor, on the other hand, earns his money by charging a percentage of the value of the assets of his client. His only concern is to increase the assets even if that means no transactions for a long period of time. As a rule, only someone with a large portfolio (over $250,000) considers an investment counselor to begin with, and a close relationship usually develops. (If it doesn't, I've been told, the investor would do well to look elsewhere.) But once a good, long-term relationship has been established, most counselors are willing to act as a home-base manager for a client exploring far horizons. One such counselor I talked to—Rick Liebley in Southern California—already has several sailors, including a live-aboard cruiser, as clients. He became intrigued with the prospect of acting as a manager for long-distance cruisers to the point of researching the possibility of setting up just such a service. Like the other professionals I interviewed, however, he still insists he would do it only for clients he knew well. And he would want a legal agreement spelling out specific duties, both for his own protection and for that of his clients.

The yellow pages of any metropolitan phone book are filled with names of investment counselors, advisors, financial planners and financial managers. It's not a good place to look for someone to handle all your money in your absence—any more than you'd stab a finger at the yellow pages to select a doctor or a dentist.

It's better to start with word-of-mouth recommendations from friends and business associates. Talk to several. Find out how long they have been in business in the same area and how successful they have been. Check the portfolios of other clients, and look for a counselor who is dealing with people who have incomes and investment goals similar to yours.

An excellent place to start a search is with your stockbroker. Ask him to recommend a counselor. Frequently large brokerage firms maintain a list of "approved" people in the community—advisors who have been checked out by the brokerage and who meet the firm's standards as reputable and experienced business people. Often a broker will recommend not one but several counselors, then sit with the client when he interviews each person to offer advice and help him reach a decision.

The title of Registered Investment Advisor (RIA) doesn't mean much. All it takes to get the title is to send $150 to the Securities and Exchange Commission (SEC) along with a sworn statement confirming you have never violated a securities law. No investigation is conducted and no exams are given.

 **Don't choose a home-base manager by stabbing at names in the yellow pages. Start instead—if someone doesn't come immediately to mind—with recommendations from friends and business associates.**

On the other hand, someone with the title Certified Financial Planner (CFP) has spent a great deal of time in study and training, and has passed a long series of tests covering all phases of financial planning and investing. A CFP is a professional.

One other point to consider is granting the power of attorney. Power of attorney is simply your authorization, in writing, for someone else (and it doesn't have to be an attorney, it can be anyone) to act in your behalf and in your name. A "general" power of attorney gives the person complete control over any business dealings at all. It is much better to give a "limited" power of attorney that spells out definite, specific rights and eliminates all others. For example, you might grant power of attorney to a friend to sell your car after you leave. But he would have no power to do anything else. Power of attorney forms can be purchased at most stationery or office supply stores.

However, if your affairs are complicated or your investments considerable, have an attorney draw up the papers to insure that all legal aspects are covered. For less-complicated arrangements—authorizing your accountant to pay bills, for instance—a simple agreement in writing should suffice and a power of attorney is not necessary.

Anyone who is paying bills or conducting other financial transactions for you will require access to your money. Decide whether you want to give them authorization to write checks on your bank account (some banks will require opening a new account, but in any case forms must be signed at the bank). If you open a separate special account, estimate how much they will need and arrange for a specific amount to be transferred each month from your regular account to the new joint account.

The bottom line for selecting anyone as an investment counselor or as a home-base manager, regardless of their profession, is that it be someone you trust and someone with whom you feel comfortable. This can only happen over a long period of time, so start establishing this relationship long before casting off docklines. Otherwise, you are better off doing it yourself, even by long distance.

Doing It Yourself

Some who escape successfully are able to simplify their lives enough so that it's easy to manage everything themselves, with the exception of mail forwarding (see Chapter Eight). They carry no insurance, have no credit cards and no investments, and earn their living as they go, taking payment in cash or opening local bank accounts.

 **Document exactly what powers of attorney you are assigning to someone in your absence.**

Even if your business affairs are a little more complicated, it still is possible to take care of them yourself. Deposits can go directly to the bank, or they can be mailed to you to deposit by mail. Envelopes are generally provided, so deposits can be mailed from anywere. Get a stash of them from the bank before leaving. Remember, though, this causes a delay, possibly a month or more. Incoming checks must still go to your mailing address and then sit around until they're forwarded (more on mail forwarding in Chapter Eight).

While opening a bank account in an area where you plan to stay awhile is a good idea, it does not guarantee instant cash if you are depositing out-of-state or out-of-country checks. Usually these checks will take two weeks, at a minimum, to clear. Even though bankers use computers and should be able to handle such transactions quickly, it just doesn't happen. In Hawaii, it took *three* weeks for my out-of-state checks to clear, and that included cashier's checks. "They can be forged, too," the bank manager told me (more on getting money in Chapter Seven).

Arrangements can be made to have payments, such as loan payments and bills for credit card charges, automatically deducted from your bank account. For several suggestions on how to handle credit card billings, which accrue high interest penalties when overdue, see the credit card section in Chapter Seven.

Insurance companies generally send out premium notices four to six weeks before they are due. That should be ample time for them to trickle through the mail service and get paid before cancellation. Check to make sure you'll have enough time.

 **You *CAN* do it yourself, particularly if you keep the number of transactions at a bare minimum. Try making up a detailed calendar so you'll know exactly when bills are due and other transactions necessary.**

Without a home-base manager, an excellent plan is to keep a calendar notebook, listing due dates for all payments and collections. It also can include items such as the date a certificate of deposit will reach maturity, when estimated tax returns are due, and a reminder to check in with a stockbroker every few months. If there's one thing I discovered that I have in common with everyone else who's ever made an escape, it's that we all have the ability to completely lose track of time. A lot of us have trouble remembering what month it is, let alone what *day*. A calendar notebook is the perfect way to jog the memory and get back in touch with the real world. Then all we have to do is remember to check the notebook on a regular basis.

A big part of escaping for many people is that it means simplifying their lives as much as possible, getting rid of cars and houses and utility bills and worrisome investments. The fewer complications you leave behind, the less you'll have to worry about after you leave.

CHAPTER SIX

Investing the Nest Egg

An escape-oriented investment strategy

A handful of escape artists earn their living as they go by writing, doing photography, making yacht deliveries, or working in boat yards, restaurants or temporary-help agencies. As my father used to say, it's often a case of chicken one day and feathers the next. But work may be easy to find in one port and all but impossible 500 miles down the road. Transients aren't always welcome. "Why should I invest the time and money to train you," employers say, "when you're going to upanchor and leave in a month or two?" It's a valid point. And work permits for U.S. citizens generally aren't easy to get in a foreign country.

It's a hardy group of vagabonds—and they are almost always very young—who can lead this type of existence, never knowing for sure where their next meal is coming from. The majority of cruising people I know have at least some money set aside to pay for the cruise, although many do *supplement* their income by odd jobs along the way. This chapter assumes a cruising fund exists—gleaned from earnings, thievery, inheritance or selling the farm. The question is, what to do with it?

Special problems exist for those who want to escape and still make the most out of their money. A big problem is communication. A telephone isn't always handy to call a stockbroker or investment counselor. I once spent three days riding out a Force 9 gale, anchored up a marshy, protected backwater just north of Charleston, South Carolina. So near to civilization, yet impossible to get ashore through the swamp, much less into Charleston itself.

A man anchored nearby was in a state of near-panic. He had been listening to stock reports on a public radio station and felt he had to get in touch with his broker. For whatever reason, he was unable to raise the marine operator on his VHF radio. The impression he conveyed was that he was ruined, or at least the cruise was ruined, if he didn't make the call. With his wife in tears, they struggled to raise their anchors and headed out into the teeth of the storm. I've often wondered how he would have fared on a long ocean passage, out of touch for weeks or months at a time.

For a relaxed escape, then, look for investments that are reasonably safe, ones that do not require constant monitoring. In investment jargon, it's called a *"low-maintenance" investment*. And while we naturally want the highest return possible, it is a fact that high yields and high risks go hand-in-hand. A savings account in a commercial bank, for instance, is safe, but the minimum return (set by federal law) is a low 5.25%. At the other end of the spectrum, speculators have made virtual killings in the commodities market, but they risked it all in doing so. Obviously, much lies in between. Table 1 illustrates returns from various types of investments over the past five years.

 **For a relaxed escape, look for investments that don't require constant monitoring.**

Another requirement for cruisers is that at least a portion of any investment portfolio be *highly liquid*. That is, you want to be able to get your hands on it quickly if the money is needed in an emergency.

One factor that everyone—at home or at sea—must deal with is inflation. Table 2 shows what inflation can do to purchasing power.

TABLE 1	**RETURN FROM INVESTMENT DOLLAR**				
Chart courtesy of Wright Investors' Service, Bridgeport, CT					
If you put your money in:	**1982***	**1981**	**1980**	**1979**	**1978**
U.S. T-Bills (90-day)	13.48%	11.45%	14.77%	9.93%	9.56%
U.S. T-Bills (180-day)	13.87	12.82	14.82	10.11	10.03
CDs (90-day)	13.70	12.63	16.50	10.00	9.13
U.S. Government Notes	13.38	14.15	13.29	9.17	9.24
U.S. Bonds (long-term)	13.81	14.16	12.06	9.02	8.94
Municipals (long-term)	12.00	12.60	9.20	5.85	6.20
Corporate Bonds (AA)	13.85	13.80	12.60	9.00	9.00
Dow Jones Industrials	6.87	6.36	5.63	6.56	6.03
Dow Jones Utilities	10.34	10.30	8.77	9.55	9.08

*Spring 1982

TABLE 2   **THE ERODING EFFECT OF TIME AND INFLATION ON THE BUYING POWER OF ONE DOLLAR**

Chart courtesy of The Thorndike Encyclopedia of Banking and Financial Tables, Warren, Gorham and Lamont Inc., Boston, MA

Years From Now	5%	6%	7%	8%	9%	10%
5	$1.28	$1.34	$1.40	$ 1.47	$ 1.54	$ 1.61
10	1.63	1.79	1.97	2.16	2.37	2.59
15	2.08	2.40	2.76	3.17	3.64	4.18
20	2.65	3.21	3.87	4.66	5.60	6.73
25	3.39	4.29	5.43	6.85	8.62	10.83
30	4.32	7.74	7.61	10.06	13.27	17.45

At an inflation rate of 6%, in five years it will take $134 to buy what $100 will buy today. In 10 years it will take $179. Rates of inflation, as anyone today knows, can change quickly and drastically.

While inflation means a rise in the cost of living, it can also apply to increasing the yield on an investment. Using Table 2 again, you can see that an investment at only 7% will increase that $100 to $140 in five years and almost double it in ten years.

Strategies for the Small Investor

With a limited amount of money—$5,000 or less—there are not a lot of choices available. *All* of your money should be easily accessible. The simplest way is to carry a small amount, a few hundred dollars perhaps, in cash and the rest in traveler's checks. A thousand dollars' worth of traveler's checks will cost $10. That means you lose money, especially considering inflation, but it's a safe way to carry money. And traveler's checks *are* highly liquid in most places.

Or, a portion can be carried aboard in cash and traveler's checks, with the balance left in a checking account.

A better way is to carry only a portion, maybe $1,000 or $2,000, in cash and traveler's checks and put the rest where it will do some work. This could be a savings account, interest-bearing checking account, or possibly a money market fund. (More on this shortly).

 **Another criteria for the escape artist's portfolio is to make investments that are highly liquid.**

The following is a description of various investment options, each judged on how well they meet the requirements of low maintenance, liquidity and ability to turn a profit.

SAVINGS ACCOUNTS

The minimum return on a savings account is fixed by federal law. A commercial bank will pay 5.25%; a savings and loan (S&L) 5.50%. This doesn't mean the total yield will be the same because all banks do not use the same method of compounding interest. Some banks pay interest only on specific dates, usually quarterly. For example, if money is deposited in August and interest isn't paid until September, the yield from that account will be substantially less than an account with a bank paying interest compounded *daily* from the date of deposit. This is the best way of compounding and it's worth it to shop around for such a bank.

All savings accounts are insured for a maximum of $100,000. Accounts in commercial banks are covered by the Federal Deposit Insurance Corporation (FDIC); S&Ls by the Federal Savings and Loan Insurance Corporation (FSLIC).

Don't assume all banks pay the same interest. And read the fine print, accounts that compound daily are best.

INTEREST-BEARING CHECKING ACCOUNTS

These accounts, commonly called NOW (Negotiable Orders of Withdrawal) accounts, pay at least the same interest as a savings account, and they are insured the same way. If the balance drops below the stated minimum, however, there is a service charge. Both the minimum balance and the service charge vary widely from bank to bank. So, like a savings account, it pays to shop around. Table 3 shows the difference between some of the banks in just one area (Orange County, California).

Like any checking account, a NOW account is completely liquid; but the money is earning interest instead of just sitting there. For someone with minimum funds, this might be a better option than a savings account, although that would depend on how long the minimum balance could be maintained before the monthly charges start eating away at the interest.

Banks also differ in the extra services provided with NOW accounts. Some offer free checks and automatic teller machines (I found this extremely useful when I cruised in Florida and had an account with a statewide bank). Others offer no minimum balance for retired people.

NOW accounts are highly liquid, but figure out when service charges will begin eating away earnings. In the long run, small sums might be better off in a simple savings account.

TABLE 3 **INTEREST-BEARING CHECKING ACCOUNTS**		
Bank	**Account**	**Minimum (No Charge)**
Bank of Newport	NOW	$2,000
	ULTRA NOW	$2,500
Bank of America	NOW	$2,000
	Investor's Checking	$5,000
Marine National Bank	NOW	$2,500
Security Pacific	Interest Bearing	$1,000
Wells Fargo	Market Rate	$2,500
Crocker National	NOW	$1,500
Pacific National	NOW	$1,500

CERTIFICATE OF DEPOSIT (CD)

CDs do not meet one of our "escape requirements" since they are not highly liquid. Thus, they are not advisable for the small ($5,000 and under) investor. The reason for this is that while there are CDs available for as little as $1,000, they are 30-month CDs and usually carry a penalty for early withdrawal.

Six-month CDs can now be purchased for $2,500, but six months is still a long time if it represents half of your investment capital, particularly in view of the early withdrawal penalties. Generally, for a CD with a maturity date of a year or longer, the penalty equals six months' interest. Those that mature in less than a year, the penalty is three months' interest. If the withdrawal occurs before that much interest has been earned, the penalty is deducted from the principal. Ouch!

In spite of this, CDs still deserve mention because they are safe (insured up to $100,000 just like savings accounts) and they provide a reasonable return. Interest rates are based on current yields of United States Treasury Bills. At this writing, T-bills are yielding, on the average, 8.5%.

Some brokerage firms sponsor unit investment trusts that allow investors to pool their money to buy CDs. The minimum investment can be as low as $1,000 for one unit of the trust.

Interest	Service Charge
5¼%	Below $1,000—$6.00 month + .15 per check
7¼%	Below $2,500—becomes NOW account
5¼%	Below $2,000—$3.00 month + .15 per check
7.7%	Below $5,000—$5.00 month
6½%	Below $2,500—$10.00 month + interest drops to 5¼
5¼%	Below $1,000—$4.00 month + .18 per check
7%	Below $2,500—$10.00 month + interest drops to 5¼
5¼%	Below $1,000—$3.50 month + .15 per check
5¼%	Below $1,500—$5.00 month + .15 per check

While in Florida, I met a couple in their early 50s who were cruising along the eastern seaboard, with occasional trips to the Bahamas. They had taken an early retirement, sold their home and now live aboard the boat year-round. With a portion of the profits from the sale of the house, they purchased several 6-month CDs, spacing the purchases over a number of months so the maturity dates would be different. As each CD matures, they withdraw the interest and add it to the cash portion of their cruising fund, then buy another CD.

Bob told me that while they both have adequate retirement incomes, the CD returns give them a nice cushion for those little extras. And he likes knowing that every few months a large chunk is available if they need it. Other investments would give higher yields, but they prefer the safety of having the money in a bank.

 **Certificates of Deposit are not liquid and are not advisable for the low-capital investor. But their high interest and low maintenance may make CDs attractive to those with bigger nest eggs.**

MONEY MARKET FUNDS

A money market fund is a special type of mutual fund. Rather than investing in common stocks, they invest only in short-term securities such as U.S. Government Treasury Bills, CDs, repurchase agreements, commercial paper and bankers' acceptances (these are known as fixed-income investments). Interest is compounded daily. These are no-load (no sales fee) funds, so *all* of your investment starts earning income right away. Yields are based on existing interest rates. If interest rates climb, the yields increase; conversely, they decrease when interest rates go down. Even when interest rates are declining, most money market funds still yield considerably more than the return from a passbook savings account. To find out current earnings of money market funds, check the financial section of any large metropolitan newspaper (like the New York *Times* or the Los Angeles *Times*) or the *Wall Street Journal*.

Money market funds are available for the small investor, some of them requiring a minimum initial investment as low as $1,000. There are a wide variety of money market funds (see Table 4 for a sampling) and, for the most part, they are a reasonably safe investment. They're not as safe as a bank account or a CD, however, since only a few are insured and there is no guarantee of a high yield. Choose a fund associated with a well-known established brokerage house—one that is investing in U.S. Government securities and short-term debts from top-rated corporations and major banks. Some of the flashier funds may be showing higher yields, but they may be taking greater risks, too, such as buying foreign CDs or commercial paper of lower-rated corporations.

Funds that invest only in U.S. Government securities offer the highest possible safety, but generally a lower yield than a more diversified money fund. And for someone in a high tax bracket, there are funds that invest in tax-exempt municipal securities.

Before buying into any fund, discuss it with a broker, and study the fund's prospectus carefully. The prospectus will describe the fund and its goals, state the services offered to shareholders (like check-writing privileges, withdrawal plans, monthly reports, etc.), and it will list all the holdings of the fund so you can see for yourself the quality of the investments.

Money market funds can be liquid, but only if arrangements are

| TABLE 4 **MONEY MARKET FUNDS**

Chart courtesy of Donoghue's MONEY MARKET REPORT

Fund	For Period Ended 4/14/82			Average Maturity (Days)
	7 Day	30 Day	12 Mo.	
U.S. TREASURY				
Capital Preservation	13.1%	13.0%	14.8%	19
Merrill Lynch Gov't	13.3	13.4	15.4	37
U.S. GOVERNMENT				
First Variable Rate	13.7	13.6	16.1	28
NRTA-AARP	13.0	12.9	15.3	34
DOMESTIC				
Alliance Capital	13.4	13.4	16.1	25
Intercapital	13.9	13.7	16.6	36
Fidelity Daily	13.8	13.7	16.4	32
Vanguard MMT Prime	13.9	13.8	16.4	26
EUROS/YANKEES				
Cash Equivalents	14.3	14.2	16.8	37
Kemper Money Mkt.	14.3	14.2	16.8	33
T. Rowe Price Reserve	14.0	14.1	16.4	26
Average Yield	13.78	13.77		
Average Maturity				30

U.S. = U.S. Government Securities; Repos = Repurchase Agreements; CDs = Certificates of Deposit; BA = Bankers' Acceptances; CP = Commercial Paper; Foreign = European CDs and Yankee $ CDs.

made in advance. Tom and Ann Selck spent ten months cruising from Lake Erie to the U.S. Virgin Islands in their 36-foot sailboat *Shamrock*. They invested in a money market fund and arranged for a specific amount to be transferred monthly to their checking account. Ann says that twice during the cruise she called her broker and had cash wired to her from the fund.

A typical fund is the Merrill Lynch Ready Assets Trust Fund (minimum investment $5,000). Under the systematic withdrawal plan, shareholders with at least a $5,000 investment can specify quarterly withdrawals. Those with at least $10,000 in the fund can elect monthly withdrawals. Aside from an automatic transfer, money can

Portfolio Holdings (%)					
U.S.	Repos	CDs	BA	CP	Foreign
83	17				
78	22				
67	33				
66	33	1			
7	2	27	14	50	
10	3	47	13	27	
		38	28	34	
	14	28	17	41	
				26	74
				29	71
5		9	1	56	34

be withdrawn at any time by either writing a check for a minimum of $500 with a checkbook provided by the fund, or by requesting a Federal Funds Transfer, which is a transfer of money by wire from the fund's bank to the shareholder's bank. But, and here's the kicker, money can *only* be wired to a pre-approved bank. You cannot simply walk into any bank in the world and have money wired to you. Any such limitations will be spelled out in the fund's prospectus.

One couple, Jack and Pat Tyler, used a Ready Assets Trust investment to finance a year's cruise with their 4-year-old son Devin aboard their sloop, *Felicity*. Since their sailing was coastal, from the Chesapeake to the Florida Keys and back to Annapolis, they were always

Before going into a money market fund, discuss the investment carefully with your broker. There are funds to suit every set of needs and practically every pocketbook. Each fund has a prospectus. Read it carefully before investing your cash.

pretty close to banks, as well as to branch offices of Merrill Lynch. When they needed additional funds, Jack would telephone his broker in Annapolis and ask him to wire money to a branch office in whatever port *Felicity* was docked at the time. Generally, by the next day, a check would be waiting at the local office. Jack would ask the cashier at Merrill Lynch which bank would cash it for him and they'd be on their way again. Merrill Lynch is in the business of investments, not banking, and they discourage this practice. But Jack says a sincere, sad voice can work wonders.

Recent changes in federal law now allow banks to offer money market accounts paying interest comparable to the funds at brokerage houses. Typical of these is the Ultramax account at Bank of Newport in California. Minimum deposit is $2,500. Investments include Treasury Bills, commercial paper, and certificates of deposit. Among the services offered are check-writing privileges and transfer of funds to other accounts, although these transactions are limited to a total of six per month.

Money market investments can be liquid, but only if arrangements are made in advance. And some plans limit the number of transactions.

CASH MANAGEMENT ACCOUNT (CMA)

For any lucky escape artist with $20,000 or more to invest, a CMA is hard to beat. The Cash Management Account is a special blend of three money market funds. Mike Nadler, vice president of Merrill Lynch in Newport Beach, California, calls the CMA its "top-of-the-line" account. It meets all of our requirements: it's relatively safe, offers good yields and it is highly liquid. Money can be invested in a securities account and in one or all three of the CMA money market funds:

- CMA MONEY FUND: Invests in U.S. Government and U.S. Government agency securities, CDs, commercial paper and other short-term money market securities.
- CMA TAX-EXEMPT FUND: Invests in short-term, tax-free municipal securities. This may be the best choice for someone in a high tax bracket.
- CMA GOVERNMENT SECURITIES FUND: Invests only in securities backed by the U.S. Government, such as Treasury Bills and repurchase agreements. This offers the highest degree of safety of the three funds.

These are all no-load funds, with dividends and interest automatically reinvested daily. Additionally, any dividends or interest earned in the securities account is automatically invested in whichever of the three funds has been designated as the primary one.

Monies in the funds can be accessed by writing a check or, more importantly for anyone far from home, by using a special VISA card supplied by Bank One of Columbus, Ohio, (one of the largest processors of VISA transactions in the country). The card can be used for cash advance at any of the 100,000 VISA banks located in 152 countries around the world, as well as at more than 3,000,000 retail establishments. A VISA bank will verify the credit line, which is done by wire. Due to time differences, this could take several hours or, at worst, 24 hours.

 Cash management accounts meet all the escape artist's investment criteria. The investment is safe, liquid, doesn't require constant monitoring and earns top interest. The only hitch: You've got to plunk down $20,000.

Unlike most other credit cards, there is no arbitrary credit limit with the CMA VISA card. The limit is determined by the value of the assets in the account. Any charges are automatically deducted each month and spelled out in the monthly statement. You won't get stung paying high interest penalties because a credit card invoice got delayed in the mail-forwarding process.

In an emergency, the same VISA card can be used to access the loan value of any marginable securities in the brokerage account portion of the CMA. Margin limits are set by federal law. With common stock, up to 50% of the market value can be borrowed; with corporate and municipal bonds, 70%. With government bonds you can borrow 92% of their market value. While few set out planning to borrow money, the knowledge that it is available if needed can add to a feeling of financial security when you're far from home.

Each month, CMA shareholders receive a comprehensive monthly statement listing all transactions in chronological order, including the names of payees on checks and VISA card purchases, together with the amounts. Also, summaries of each type of transaction are provided: VISA charges, interest and dividends earned, securities bought and sold and the latest value of all holdings in the account. At the present time, Merrill Lynch charges an annual $50 fee for the CMA service.

Among the accounts that are almost identical to Merrill Lynch's CMA are the Asset Managment Account offered by E. F. Hutton and the Active Assets Account available from Dean Witter Reynolds. The Active Assets uses a VISA card and Hutton's AMA an American Express Gold Card. E. F. Hutton charges an annual fee of $80, while Dean Witter Reynolds charges $30 a year.

Considering all the advantages, liquidity through check writing, the international credit card, a reasonable amount of safety, automatic daily reinvestment of interest and dividends, professional advice from an account executive, timely payment of credit card charges, the convenience of all activities handled in one account, and a monthly statement of all transactions, this type of account seems to be tailor-made for the cruising sailor or anyone taking off on an extended escape.

STOCKS

Investing in quality stocks offers a better chance than a money market fund for high yields but, as mentioned earlier, the risks are higher, too. One of the biggest problems for anyone far from home is time. It takes time to keep track of market trends, to study financial reports and business papers, to research stocks before investing and to review them every few months after investing. Anyone playing the stock market must be in a position to act quickly.

Still, anyone with more than $20,000 might want to consider putting part of it into low-risk stocks, or into high-grade bonds. Remember, too, that such securities can be part of a cash management-type account.

One type of low-risk investment suggested by several brokers is utility stocks—stocks in publicly-owned utilities such as Southern California Edison. Yields on good grade utilities are now in the range of 10–11%. The risk is that the price of the stock could go down as well as up, although it is still a low risk. Southern California Edison, for example, has increased its dividend payments for seven of the last ten years, and that's typical of a quality utility stock.

For those in a high income tax bracket (35% and up), investing in common stock can have advantages. Under today's tax laws, all income is taxed at the highest rate, but only 40% of income from long-term capital gains is taxed. Capital gains applies to stocks that have been held for at least 12 months. As an example, someone in the 45% tax bracket will pay .45 of every dollar earned as a dividend, but only .18 on every dollar earned as capital gains. Stocks chosen for a long-term capital-gain investment should be high quality stocks in profitable and growing companies. Ask your broker for recommendations. Look at financial publications like Standard & Poor's *Stock Guide*, *Barron's*, *Forbes* or one of the many investment market letters. Research promising-looking companies by studying their financial reports, their latest prospectus (required by the Securities and Exchange Commission (SEC) for every over-the-counter stock), and their market track record. But keep in mind that stocks purchased for a long-term investment can no longer be considered highly liquid. Sell them too soon and all profits will be taxed at the highest rate.

 **Stocks are not the best investment for anyone far from home or likely to be out of touch. An exception to this rule of thumb might be investing in the stock of a high-grade public utility.**

I do know two couples who cruised for several years (one couple completed a circumnavigation) and supported themselves entirely on dividends and interest from common stocks and bonds. Both couples had investments of more than $100,000 and both had trusted financial advisors who handled their portfolios (see Chapter Four). A good idea for someone in this position who wants a steady cash flow is to choose a number of stocks by the months in which they pay quarterly dividends. Pick several that pay in January, April, July and October, for instance, another group that pays in February, May, August and November, and a third group that pays in March, June, September and December.

Investors with only a small amount of cash but who are intrigued by the stock market and who have several years to work at it before escaping can get started with as little as $25 in programs such as Merrill Lynch's Sharebuilder Plan. This is not a mutual fund where stock purchases are the decision of the fund's management. In the Sharebuilder Plan, each investor chooses his own stocks, and the orders are combined with other Sharebuilder orders so the firm can buy and sell in quantity. This allows each investor to purchase fractions of shares as a way of getting started. Commission rates are discounted up to 40% on transactions under $5,000. Dividends are automatically reinvested. And the plan is liquid—shares can be sold at any time. Additionally, Merrill Lynch will supply a list of stock recommendations to investors.

BONDS

Bonds are another low-risk investment. Buying a bond is essentially buying a debt. The investor is making a loan (to a government or a corporation) that is repaid at a fixed rate of interest and at a set period of time. Bond values are tied to the interest rate. Since the repayment is a fixed amount, with rising interest rates the profits will erode each year. When interest rates climb, the value of bonds goes down. Bonds are not always a good hedge against inflation, but they do give a secure rate of return.

Corporate bonds are rated based on the present financial condition and the corporation's track record. For a safe investment, buy only high grade bonds with triple-A or double-A ratings. Corporate bonds are traded on the market just like stocks and their price varies daily, although the swing is seldom as much as common stock.

The safest fixed-income investment is a government security—direct obligations of the United States Treasury. As long as the U.S. government is around, investors will receive their interest payments like clockwork. Treasury *Bills* require a minimum investment of $10,000 and are available in maturities of three, six, nine and 12 months. Treasury *Notes* can be purchased for $1,000 and with maturity dates of one to ten years. Treasury *Bonds* also start at $1,000 but maturity is from ten to 25 years.

One of the most popular government-guaranteed bonds today is a "Ginnie Mae" (GNMA)—a Government National Mortgage Association bond. Yields on Ginnie Maes are the highest of any of the Treasury obligations. A Ginnie Mae holder in effect owns a share in a pool of FHA and VA mortgages, and receives a monthly payment of principal and interest. Since these are mortgages, early payments are primarily interest. As the bond amortizes the interest portion is reduced but the total monthly payment remains the same. When a mortgage is paid off (usually because the owner refinances or sells the house) the Ginnie Mae holder receives an extra payment based on the percentage of his holdings and subsequent monthly payments are re-

TABLE 5   **FIXED-INCOME SECURITIES**

Chart courtesy of *The Complete Bond Book* by David M. Darst

Type	Minimum Purchase	Maturity Range
SHORT TERM		
U.S. Treasury Bills	$ 10,000*	3-12 mos.
Local Authorities	1,000	3-12 mos.
FNMA notes**	50,000	30-270 days
Federal Intermediate Credit	5,000	270 days
State/Local Govt. Notes	5,000	1-12 mos.
Bankers' Acceptances	5,000	1-270 days
Negotiable CDs	100,000	1-12 mos.
CDs	10,000	1 year
	1,000	30 mos.
Commercial Paper	100,000	1-270 days
MEDIUM TERM		
U.S. EE Bonds	25	9 years
U.S. HH Bonds	500	10 years
U.S. Treasury Notes/Bonds	1,000	1-30 years
Federal Financing Bank Notes/Bonds	1,000	1-20 years
FHA Notes/Certificates	25,000	1-25 years
GNMA Securities/Certificates***	5,000	1-25 years
GNMA pass-throughs***	25,000	14-17 years
Federal Land Bank Bonds	1,000	1-10 years
Corporate Notes/Bonds	1,000	1-30 years
Eurobond Bonds/Notes	1,000	3-25 years

*On discount basis; with 1 year, $10,000 bill @ 15% = +$8,500
**Federal National Mortgage Association
***Government National Mortgage Association

duced. The interest portion of the monthly payment is taxable income but the balance is non-taxable return of capital. Buying into a Ginnie Mae generally costs about $25,000, but some brokerage firms sponsor funds with shares costing as little as $1,000 each.

Municipal bonds are issued by state and local governments. Interest earned on them is exempt from federal income tax, and frequently it is exempt from state income tax as well. They can be a good investment for someone in a high tax bracket (over 35%), since they will net more money even though the bond will yield slightly less than a

Liquidity	Interest	Where Available
Best	Discount*	Banks, Brokers, Federal Reserve Banks, AMEX
Average	Straight	Banks, Brokers
Good	Discount	Major Dealers
Good	Straight	Banks, Brokers
Average	Straight	Banks, Brokers
Average	Discount	Banks, Brokers
Average	Straight	Banks, Brokers
Penalty/early withdrawal	Straight, Compounded	Banks, S&Is, Credit Unions
See above	See above	See above
Average	Straight	Dealers
Poor	Discount	Banks, US Treasury
Penalty/early withdrawal	Straight	Federal Reserve
Good	Straight	Banks, Brokers
Good	Straight	Banks, Brokers
Average	Straight	Banks, Brokers
Average	Straight	Banks, Brokers
Good	Straight	Banks, Brokers
Good	Straight	Banks, Brokers
Good	Straight	Brokers
Average	Straight	Foreign Banks

taxable one. People in lower tax brackets will do better buying higher yielding bonds and paying the tax. Also, municipal bonds should not be considered a liquid asset. C. Colburn Hardy, in his book *Dun & Bradstreet's Guide to $Your Investments$*, cautions that only those who can afford to invest a minimum of $5,000 and hold the investment for several years, preferably to maturity, should consider tax-exempt bonds.

Table 5 shows the many types of bonds available, along with other fixed-income securities, so you can compare minimum purchase

> The safest fixed income investment for the escape artist are U.S. Treasury Notes, Bills and Bonds. But they will tie up your money from three months to 25 years.

prices and degree of liquidity.

MUTUAL FUNDS

"Mutual funds" is the term most often used in reference to investment companies. In strictest terms, it is the correct name for *open-end* investment companies—that use shareholders' money to invest in securities of other corporations but whose share values are fixed in direct proportion to the net worth of the company at any given time. *Closed-end* funds, on the other hand, usually are listed on the major stock exchanges and have a specific number of shares that are bought and sold like common stocks.

For the escape investor who wants to enter the stock market, investment companies are generally a better way to go then playing the market on their own. Hardy says, "Unless you have ready access to current statistical information and can devote many hours to studying the economy, the stock market, industries and specific stocks, investment companies will get you results that are as good as, and usually better than, what you can achieve on your own." He adds that it's almost impossible to achieve a properly balanced portfolio with less than a $50,000 minimum. With an investment company, the small investor can get a good diversification plus the advantage of professional management.

There are basically two types of mutual funds—load funds and no-load funds. Load funds are sold by fund salespeople or brokerage firms, and a sales fee is charged—usually about 8½% of the amount invested. No-load funds are sold by the mutual fund itself, with no sales charge. Both types of funds charge an annual management fee, usually ½% to 1%. As a rule of thumb, figure that a load fund must produce about 1% higher earnings than a no-load fund to get the same yield.

 **For the small investor escaping from everything except the stock market, mutual funds may be the safest, most profitable investment.**

There exist approximately 500 mutual funds to choose from. The research in picking the right fund is similar to choosing stocks: look for a well-managed, profitable and growing fund with a good track record. Study the prospectus, annual reports and financial statements, and get a copy of the annual mutual fund report produced by *Forbes* magazine, which rates funds according to past performance. Among the types of funds available are:

- GROWTH FUND: Investments chosen for long-term capital gains instead of dividends. Emphasis is on common stock.
- INCOME FUND: Invests in securities that pay high yields, such as income-producing common stocks and corporate bonds.
- BALANCED FUND: Invests in quality common stocks and fixed-income securities for some growth potential with a fairly safe investment base.
- TAX-EXEMPT FUND: Invests in municipal bonds paying tax-exempt income.

Mutual funds can be set up to provide income on a regular basis. Dividends are usually paid quarterly, but they can be spread out in monthly payments. Another plan could be to buy into several funds that pay dividends in different months. For the investor with less cash to put to use, arrangements can sometimes be made to sell a certain portion of shares each month to assure a steady escape income.

REAL ESTATE

A lot of people sell their homes when they take off, using the money to pay off the boat or camper or investing it to finance the escape. An alternative is to keep the house, lease or rent it, and live off that income. When George and Doris Hubbard, both age 55, went cruising for 16 months on their 37-foot sailboat, their only debt was a $216 monthly house payment. They leased the house for $416 a month, covering their payment and giving them $200 income. This, added to income from part-ownership in a commercial building and interest income from their savings gave them a total income of $1,000 a month —a comfortable cruising budget.

The biggest worry with rental property, particularly if it's a single-family dwelling, is that it stays rented every month. Wayne and Kris Carpenter spent three years on a circumnavigation of the North Atlantic aboard *Marie Rose*, a 32-foot wood ketch. They lived on rental income from a mortgaged house in California. Wayne says that was the biggest risk they took. He lived in fear of a month's vacancy, since he did not have the resources to cover any missed payments by his tenants. But it didn't worry him enough not to do it again. Their second cruise, on the 27-foot *Kristina*, was financed primarily by rental income, although by then Wayne was earning additional money through his writing (and, he claims, by selling beads to Caribbean natives!).

 **If you've got real estate, keeping it and leasing it may be the soundest investment, especially if it's paid for or if it carries a low-interest mortgage.**

Meeting a mortgage payment is not the only expense in owning real estate. Property taxes must be considered, as well as maintenance and repair costs. And unless you know the tenants very well, there is the added headache of wondering how well they are caring for the property in your absence. This can be overcome by hiring a rental agent or property manager but that, too, is an additional expense unless your manager is a trusted relative or good friend.

Retirement

Along the way I've met many couples cruising comfortably on retirement income—either from long-term investments they had made early on, from individual retirement plans like IRA and Keogh funds, or from company-sponsored pension plans.

Anyone planning an early retirement should consider a few points. If you work for a company with a retirement program, investigate the plan carefully before turning in your resignation. Find out how long you must be employed there before benefit rights are vested (guaranteed even if you quit). Minimum standards for vested rights were set by the Employee Retirement Security Act of 1974. Some plans now allow partial vesting after only five years of employment and full vesting after only ten years. It may be advantageous to postpone your escape for a year or so if you are that close to partial or total vesting. Investigate the vesting portion of any profit-sharing plan you may be part of.

Some companies will pay a lump-sum from the pension plan if an employee quits or retires early. If these funds are "rolled over" into an IRA retirement account within 60 days, no income tax will have to be paid.

 **There's no doubt about it, the best time to escape may be when you retire, particularly if you're enrolled in a healthy retirement fund.**

Early retirement, of course, doesn't necessarily mean income will start rolling in immediately. IRA and Keogh plans don't start to pay until age 59½. Corporate pension plans vary—some start as early as 50, usually with reduced income, and others not until 63 or 65. Jan Wendland took an early retirement from his New York teaching position to go cruising. Even though vested, he has to wait five years before receiving any income. So he cruises most of the year (last year a singlehanded crossing to Europe) and works during the summer as an instructor at the Outward Bound School in Maine. While in Europe he added to his cruising fund by giving skiing lessons.

The Golden Rule: Plan Ahead

There are myriad ways of investing money to finance your escape, not all of them suitable for everyone. The single overriding factor is how well you sleep at night. One broker calls it "risk tolerance." Whatever we call it, different people have different levels. Some enjoy the excitement of playing the stock market, taking chances for quick profits. Others are only happy with money tucked safely away in their neighborhood savings and loan.

 **Ultimately, the most important criteria for your escape investment strategy is how well you'll sleep at night.**

Before making any investment, examine your own needs and goals, then talk over your plans with a competent professional—a banker, stockbroker, investment counselor, attorney or accountant (or all of the above). Earl Hinz, author of *Sail Before Sunset* and *Landfalls of Paradise—The Guide to Pacific Islands* says, "Probably more cruises are cut short because of poor financial planning than anything else, including divorce and other personal problems."

The time involved in good planning is well worth the effort. Do it now, before you leave, to lay the foundation for a relaxing, free-from-money-worries escape.

GLOSSARY

Banker's acceptance: An obligation, secured by a real transaction, that a bank must honor on maturity.

Bond, municipal: Tax-exempt bonds issued by state and local governments. Interest earned is exempt from federal tax, and also is exempt from state taxes in the state where the bond originates.

Bond, taxable: A certificate of loan to a government or company, repaid with interest at a fixed rate and within a fixed period of time.

Capital gains: Profits earned from the sale of securities, real property or capital assets.

Capital market: The long-term debt and equity market, including stocks and bonds.

Certificate of Deposit (CD): Short-term debt issued by a bank. On maturity, the bank pays the face value of the CD plus interest. Interest rates are based on current yields of U.S. Treasury Bills.

Commercial paper: Negotiable short-term promissory notes issued by large corporations.

Common stock: Any capital stock, other than preferred stock. Preferred stock receives income before dividends are paid on common stocks.

Compound interest: Interest earned on a combination of the original investment plus unpaid accrued interest. Compounding is basically earning interest on interest.

Inflation: An increase in the amount of available money and credit that causes rising prices and a decline of currency value.

Investment company: Commonly called mutual funds, a company selling shares to many people and investing the funds in diversified securities.

Margin: Amount paid by a client who buys securities with the stockbroker's credit.

Money market: The short-term debt market, such as certificates of deposit, U.S. Government Treasury Bills, commercial paper, and bankers' acceptances.

Mutual fund: Term commonly applied to an investment company, a company selling shares to many people and investing the funds in diversified securities.

Securities: Stocks or bonds.

Short-term securities: Generally refers to securities that reach maturity in less than two years.

Yield: Interest or dividends paid on an investment, and usually expressed as a percentage. For example, a share of stock selling for $15 and paying a dividend of $1.50 would yield 10%.

CHAPTER SEVEN

Keeping the Cash Flowing

*How to cash a check in Timbuktu
and other exotic places*

As many different ways exist to handle money while away from home as there are people making escapes. Some use credit cards almost exclusively, others carry traveler's checks and nothing else. But regardless of the system used, it is a fact that money is needed no matter where you go; and when the larder's empty and there's not a nickel on the boat, getting money *is* the number one priority.

You Can't Take it All With You

For weekend and vacation cruising, even vacations that last a month or two, it is easiest to just take along all the money you will need in cash and traveler's checks. But for longer escapes, other arrangements must be made.

The best place to start is by keeping a checking account open at your own local bank. (See Chapter Six for information on interest-bearing checking accounts.) Arrangements can be made for a specified sum to be transferred each month from a savings account to a checking account. Other arrangements can be made with a stockbroker to deposit interest and dividends into your checking account or with tenants to deposit rent checks. Virtually all money that is owed you, whether from investments, book royalties, retirement plans, second trust deed on a house, or social security, can be sent directly to your bank. All this takes time, so start making arrangements several months before departure. Make sure everyone has *written* instructions on exactly how they are to handle such payments.

It pays to cultivate a strong friendship with someone in upper management (senior manager, president, vice president) at a small local bank. Chereese Smoot, who cruised with her husband throughout Mexico and the South Pacific aboard a 37-foot trimaran and is now chief financial officer at a bank in Orange, California, highly recommends this. She said when a bank officer gets to know you and understands what you are doing and the problems you might encounter, he or she will be more willing to help and will be more receptive when you call with an urgent request. She suggests a small bank because major banks tend to change managers too often. Your friendly local banker likely will still be there a year or two down the road.

Wayne Carpenter, an experienced crsuising sailor, agrees. He spent several years developing a strong professional relationship with his savings and loan manager. Wayne says he always received excellent, prompt service and that his friend would inevitably go out of her way to insure that his requests were followed.

 **Make sure everyone handling your money back home has _written_ instructions on how to handle the cash in their care.**

Arrangements also can be made with a bank to automatically take care of such things as loan payments, insurance premiums, child support payments and sometimes credit card charges.

Cash—How Much to Carry in What Form?

It's not a good idea to carry a lot of cash with you—$500 to $1,000 is about the maximum. Carry it in small denominations, mostly tens and twenties. Stores in small towns and villages may not have enough cash to make change for large-denomination bills. I even had trouble once in Newport, Rhode Island (hardly a small town), going to three different stores before I could break a $100 bill.

 **Cultivate a strong friendship with someone in upper management in your local bank. Their help in long-distance transactions could prove invaluable.**

Flashing large amounts of money around in a poverty-stricken area is bad policy anyway—an invitation to theft, or a rise in price because a store clerk sees you as one of those "rich Americans."

All the cruising people I know have found hiding places on their boats where they can secret away reserve cash. On one of my previous boats, several of the lockers had false bottoms that were virtually impossible to detect. Of course, thieves can be clever, too. Wayne and Kris Carpenter had several hiding places aboard *Kristina*. Since they built her themselves, they even included a special secret compartment.

Nevertheless, they were burglarized while at anchor at St. Georges, Grenada. He and Kris were ashore at the yacht club attending a wedding. On their return, they found the boat a complete mess. The thief had gone through the boat looking for clever hiding places (Wayne says some of them were, too), eventually finding a two-inch thick roll of bills in a very obvious place—a purse hanging in the forepeak. The theft occurred after dark, and Wayne still laughs when he thinks about how the thief must have reacted when he discovered he had actually stolen a roll of play money belonging to Wayne's daughter. Ironically, the thief was so intent on finding secret places that he overlooked $80 in U.S. currency sitting in an ashtray on the salon table.

Wayne suggests deliberately using play money as a decoy. Wrap a five-dollar bill around the roll and plant several in different "hiding places."

Lin and Larry Pardey, who cruised around the world for nine years aboard their 24-foot *Seraffyn*, kept a separate reserve of $400-$500 in small bills secreted away. In her book *The Care and Feeding of the Offshore Crew*, Lin mentions the money came in handy on several occasions. Bribery is a way of life in Egypt. They had to pay off the pilot—in cash—in order to transit the Suez Canal. She adds there were times in the Mideast when banks were boycotting certain brands of traveler's checks, and the cash reserve carried them over.

U.S. currency can be used in a surprising number of out-of-the-way places. This is particularly true in countries close to the United States frequented by American tourists, such as Mexico, Canada and the Bahamas. But here again, use small denominations because change will be in local currency. Before leaving a foreign country, try to spend any coins you've collected. While banks will exchange paper currency, they often won't handle coins.

You Can't Beat Traveler's Checks

Most cruisers carry small amounts of cash, and from $1,000–$2,000 in traveler's checks. American Express is the most common, although Earl Hinz has used Visa traveler's checks as well as American Express throughout the South Pacific and never had a problem with either. Like carrying cash, take only small denominations—mostly twenties and certainly nothing larger than fifty; it's just too hard to cash anything larger in many places.

 **As a decoy, wrap a $5 bill around a roll of play money and put it in an obvious "hiding" place.**

Be sure that each crew member has checks in his or her own name. It's not likely the same person will always be going ashore or be in need of money.

Traveler's checks cost 1% of the face value of the check. Occasionally a hotel or retail shop will charge a fee for cashing the check, especially if you are just cashing it and haven't made a purchase.

Getting Money From Home: Postal Money Orders

Postal money orders are a good way of having money sent to you, provided you are in the United States and there is someone back home with access to your bank account who is willing to handle the details. The money order fees are:

$ 1–$ 25 money order: $ .75
$25–$ 50 money order: $1.10
$50–$500 money order: $1.55

Before leaving New York for a cruise down the Intracoastal Water-way to the Bahamas, I opened a joint checking account with a trusted friend, Al Rivoire. At that time he also was handling my mail. When I called or sent a card with the address of the next post office, he could buy a money order and include it with the mail packet. This was very convenient since the mail went to general delivery. I could open the mail and cash the money order on the spot.

A word of warning, though: don't go to the post office early in the morning. Small-town post offices start the day with a limited amount of cash for making change, and they won't wipe out their reserve to cash a big money order. Wait until mid-afternoon.

There exists such a thing as an international postal money order for sending money outside the U.S. But it is not worth the time and effort it takes to buy one, and fees are higher than domestic money orders. You can't simply walk into a post office and buy one. After placing an order, it is sent to Chicago for processing, then returned to the local post office, and *then* it can be picked up. Every postal employee I spoke with said it took "a long time" (no one would say *how* long) and recommended going to a bank for a cashier's check, instead.

 **Carry your spending money in small denominations. Big bills are hard to cash and leave you with lots of change in a foreign currency that you may not need.**

Private Services: Western Union

Money can be wired via Western Union and it *is* fast. In the United States, money is wired from one Western Union office to another, without going through a bank. Often you pick up money in just a few hours. However, it's expensive: $30.95 to wire $1,000 and $23.95 to send $500. And, like money orders, someone is needed on the home-front to do the legwork—go to the bank for cash, then drive to a Western Union office to send it off.

If the office is large enough, it is possible to get cash on the spot.

Otherwise, they will type out a check and direct you to a bank that will cash it. The bank will always be within walking distance of the Western Union office. Sometimes a bank is better, anyway. I remember picking up $1,000 in Miami, Florida. I took the bus from the harbor and found the Western Union office located in a slum section near the Miami River. A half-dozen unsavory-looking characters were standing around inside the office and all eyes watched as the clerk counted out ten $100 bills for me. I fled the office and waited nervous as a cat for the return bus. I would have felt much more comfortable in the quiet privacy of a bank. And I had to go to a bank anyway, to change the hundreds into smaller bills.

 **Don't let anyone talk you into using an international postal money order. They take a long time and cost more than the domestic variety.**

Money can be wired Western Union to foreign countries, but the cost is higher and the money does not go from office to office. It is routed through Chase Manhattan Bank in New York and then to a bank in the foreign country. It is easier, faster, and will cost less to wire money from your own local bank and not bother going through Western Union.

Western Union will guarantee the arrival of money to most, but not all, countries. At this writing, they no longer guarantee anything going into Mexico: You pays your money, you takes your chances!

The Ins and Outs of Bank Transfers

The best way to receive a large lump sum of money in a foreign port is undoubtedly a bank transfer. But the system is not without its problems. Our wonderful computerized age notwithstanding, I don't know of anyone who has used bank transfers and not experienced difficulty or delays at least once. The biggest problem stems from the sheer number of banks involved. The wire travels from the local bank in the States to a major U.S. international bank, then to a major bank in the foreign country and *then* to the local foreign bank. Bank officer Chereese Smoot says it can take as long as one or two weeks, sometimes even longer.

Problems are not limited to foreign banks. I once went to a small bank in Hilton Head, South Carolina, and arranged for money to be wired from my bank in Oyster Bay, New York. The money didn't arrive and it took close to two weeks to figure out what had happened. My bank in Oyster Bay sent the transfer through Chase Manhattan in New York City. Chase Manhattan sent it to a major bank in Charleston, South Carolina, which in turn sent it to *their* branch bank in Hilton Head, located right across the street from the bank I had chosen. And there the check sat, waiting for me to pick it up.

Several things can be done to ease the way. Despite my earlier statements about the advantages of dealing with a small, local bank, this is one instance where it might be advantageous to have an account with a large international bank, such as Bank of America, Barclays or Wells Fargo (see Table 1 for a list), thus eliminating one bank from the chain. If your bank has a branch office wherever you happen to be, the whole process will be much simpler, since you'll only be working with two banks, thereby eliminating several chances for a foul-up.

Sy Carkhuff, who spent five years on a circumnaviagtion with his wife Vicki and young son David aboard their Bermuda 40 *Resolve*, says the longest delay he ever experienced was four days, and the quickest he ever received his money was 48 hours. He always waited until they were in a port that was a major banking center before having money transferred, and he stresses the importance of *getting there* first. He would pick out a major international bank and ask them which specific bank in the United States they dealt with, then note the address, telex number and any other pertinent information. He found that doing the legwork himself and transmitting as many details as possible to his local bank back in the States eliminated most chances of error.

Charges for bank transfers vary from bank to bank, although as a general rule they are less than wiring money through Western Union.

| TABLE 1 | **MAJOR INTERNATIONAL BANKS WITH OFFICES IN THE UNITED STATES**   The address shown is the bank's U.S. Headquarters. However, all have branch offices throughout the United States. |

Barclays Bank International Limited
100 Water Street
New York, NY 10005

Foreign countries with offices:

Anguilla, Antigua, Argentina, Australia, Bahamas, Barbados, Belgium, Belize, Bequia, Bermuda, Botswana, Brazil, Cameroun, Canada, Carriacou, Cayman Islands, Cyprus, Denmark, Egypt, Fiji, France, Germany, Federal Republic of Ghana, Gibraltar, Greece, Grenada, Guyana, Hong Kong, Indonesia, Iran, Ireland, Italy, Ivory Coast, Jamaica, Japan, Kenya, Korea, Republic of, Lebanon, Lesotho, Malawi, Malaysia, Malta, Mauritus, Mexico, Montsem, Netherlands, Netherlands Antilles, Nevis, New Hebrides, New Zealand, Nigeria, Philippines, Rhodesia, Rodrigues Island, St. Kitts, St. Vincent, Seychelles, Sierra Leone, Singapore, South Africa, South West Africa (Namibia), Spain, Swaziland, Switzerland, Tobago, Turkey, Turks & Caicos Islands, Uganda, Union Island, United Arab Emirates, United Kingdom, United States of America, USSR, Virgin Islands (Britain & United States), Zaire, Zambia

Manufacturers Hanover Trust Company
350 Park Avenue
New York, NY 10022

Foreign countries with offices:

REGION—1

Austria, Belgium, Bermuda, Canada, Cyprus, France, Greece, Germany, Ireland, Italy, Liechtenstein, Luxembourg, Malta, Netherlands, Switzerland, United Kingdom

REGION—3

Bulgaria, Czechoslovakia, Denmark, Finland, German Democratic Republic, Hungary, Iceland, Israel, Norway, Poland, Romania, Sweden, Turkey, U.S.S.R., Yugoslavia

REGION—2

Algeria, Bahrain, East Africa, Egypt, Indian Ocean, Iraq, Jordan, Kuwait, Lebanon, Libya, Mauritania, Morocco, Oman, Qatar, Saudi Arabia, Somalia, Southern Africa, Sudan, Syria, Tunisia, United Arab Emirates, West Africa, Yemen

REGION—4

Australia, China, Hong Kong, Japan, Korea, New Zealand, Oceania, Papua—New Guinea, Taiwan

REGION—5

Afghanistan, Bangladesh, Brunei, Burma, India, Indonesia, Iran, Khmer Republic, Laos, Malaysia, Maldives, Nepal, Pakistan, Philippines, Singapore, Sri Lanka, Thailand, Vietnam

REGION—6

Caribbean, Central America, Colombia, Mexico, Panama, Portugal, Spain, Venezuela

REGION—7

Argentina, Bolivia, Brazil, Chile, Ecuador, Paraguay, Peru, Uruguay

Chemical Bank
20 Pine Street
New York, NY 10005

Foreign countries with offices:

Argentina, Australia, Austria, Bahamas, Bahrain, Belgium, Brazil, Canada, Colombia, Egypt, France, Germany, Hong Kong, India, Indonesia, Italy, Ivory Coast, Japan, Korea, Lebanon, Mexico, Philippines, Singapore, Spain, Switzerland, Taiwan, Thailand, United Arab Emirates, United Kingdom, Venezuela

Citibank
New York, NY

Foreign countries with offices:

Adu Dhabi, Argentina, Australia (Representative Office), Austria, Bahama Islands, Bahrain, Barbados, Belgium, Bolivia, Brazil, Brunei, Canada, Cayman Islands, Chile, China, Republic of, Colombia (Representative Office), Denmark, Dominican Republic, Dubai, Ecuador, Egypt, El Salvador, Finland (Representative Office), France, Gabon, Germany, Greece, Guam, Guatemala (Representative Office), Haiti, Honduras, Hong Kong, India, Indonesia, Ireland, Italy, Ivory Coast, Jamaica, Japan, Jordan, Kenya, Korea, Lebanon, Liberia, Luxembourg, Malaysia, Mauritius, Mexico, Monaco, Morocco, Netherlands, Netherlands Antilles, New Zealand (Representative Office), Nicaragua, Niger, Norway (Representative Office), Oman, Pakistan, Panama, Paraguay, Peru, Philippines, Portugal (Representative Office), Puerto Rico, Qatar, Ras Al Khaimah, Saudi Arabia, Senegal, Sharjah, Singapore, South Africa, Spain, Sri Lanka, Sudan, Sweden (Representative Office), Switzerland, Taiwan, Thailand, Trinidad and Tobago, Tunisia, Turkey (Representative Office), United Kingdom, Uruguay, U.S.S.R. (Representative Office), Venezuela, Virgin Islands, Yemen Arab Republic, Zaire

TABLE 1 **MAJOR INTERNATIONAL BANKS (cont.)**

Bankers Trust Company
280 Park Avenue
New York, NY

Foreign countries with offices:

Bahamas, Bahrain, France, Italy, Japan, Korea, Panama, Singapore, United Kingdom, Germany, Greece, Netherlands, Spain, Portugal, Australia, Hong Kong, India, Indonesia, Philippines, Taiwan, Thailand, Argentina, Brazil, Chile, Colombia, Mexico, Venezuela, Nigeria, Tunisia, Canada

Bank of America
37-41 Broad Street
New York, NY 10004

Foreign countries with offices:

Argentina, Australia, Austria, Bahrain, Belgium, Bolivia, Brunei, Canada, Cayman Islands, Channel Islands, Chile, Costa Rica, Denmark, Dominican Republic, Ecuador, Egypt, El Salvador, France, Germany, Greece, Guam, Guatemala, Honduras, Hong Kong, India, Indonesia, Ireland, Italy, Jamaica, Japan, Korea, Lebanon, Luxembourg, Malaysia, The Netherlands, Netherlands Antilles, Nicaragua, Pakistan, Panama, Paraguay, Peru, Philippines, Puerto Rico, Singapore, Spain, Switzerland, Taiwan, Thailand, Trust Territories of Pacific Islands (Majuro, Marshall Islands, Saipan, Northern Marianas, Truk, Caroline Islands), Tunisia, United Kingdom, Uruguay, Virgin Islands, West Indies

The First National Bank of Boston
100 Federal Street
Boston, Massachusetts 02110

Foreign countries with offices:

Argentina, Bahamas, Bolivia, Brazil, Chile, France, Germany, Haiti, Hong Kong, Japan, Panama, Paraguay, Singapore, United Kingdom, Uruguay, Australia, Guatemala, Iran, Mexico, Spain, Venezuela

The First National Bank of Chicago
One First National Plaza
Chicago, Illinois 60670

Foreign countries with offices:

Canada, Haiti, Jamaica, Brazil, Mexico, Panama, Venezuela, Belgium, France, Germany, Greece, Italy, Poland, Spain, Switzerland, Ireland, Sweden, United Kingdom, Channel Islands, Scotland, Wales, Egypt, Iran, Kenya, Lebanon, Nigeria, United Arab Emirates, Australia, Hong Kong, Indonesia, Japan, Korea, Philippines, Singapore

Continental Bank
Continental Illinois National Bank and Trust Company of Chicago
231 South LaSalle Street
Chicago, Illinois 60693

Foreign countries with offices:

United Kingdom, France, Bahamas, Germany, Greece, Italy, Japan, Korea, The Netherlands, Singapore, Taiwan, Austria, Belgium, Canada, Africa, Argentina, Australia, Brazil, Colombia, Indonesia, Mexico, Philippines, Spain, Switzerland, Venezuela

Wells Fargo Bank
420 Montgomery Street
San Francisco, CA 94104

Foreign countries with offices:

Argentina, Australia, Bahamas, Brazil, Chile, Colombia, Denmark, England, France, Germany, Hong Kong, Indonesia, Japan, Korea, Mexico, Philippines, Singapore, Venezuela, Canada

Security Pacific National Bank
333 South Hope Street
Los Angeles, CA 90071

Foreign countries with offices:

Bahrain, Germany, Philippines, Singapore, England, Bahamas, Japan, Argentina, Colombia, Brazil, Australia, Panama, Mexico, Korea, Taiwan, France

 **Don't ever flash money around overseas. At best the storekeeper will label you a "rich American" and charge twice the going rate.**

The Art of Cashing Personal Checks

Once you leave home port, it is difficult to cash a personal check. A check guarantee card can help, but it won't work everywhere. Puerto Rico, for example, a U.S. possession, requires a 9-day waiting period to process U.S. checks, including cashier's checks; although if a bank manager gets to know you, he sometimes will make an exception. Bankers in small towns are more apt to be sympathetic than those in big cities.

Marinas and campgrounds sometimes will cash small checks after you have stayed there for awhile; and when you get to know some of the local people in an area, ask someone for an introduction to the manager of the neighborhood bank.

All cruising folk eventually stop and stay put for awhile. It happens for any number of reasons: to refit the boat and get ready for the next passage, to find jobs and replenish the kitty, or just because they like the place. It then makes sense to open a local bank account. When we were in Florida, I opened a checking account with Sun First National, which has more than 30 branch offices throughout the state. I was able to cash a check in almost every port we stopped.

Of all the offshore cruisers I talked to, only one—Wayne Carpenter —did not use bank transfers by wire to receive money in a foreign port. Wayne had his hometown savings and loan manager mail him cashier's checks made out for $1,000. He found it easier to cash the checks overseas than in the U.S. On his next cruise, he said, following an incident in the Canary Islands, he will have the checks sent in pairs of $500 each. Just prior to setting off across the Atlantic, he cashed a $1,000 check. The bankers would only give him the money in pesetas. Since he and Kris were totally out of money and needed stores for the crossing, they accepted the pesetas, sailed with most of them left over, and lost $100 in the exchange upon landfall in Bequia. Checks in smaller amounts would have eliminated the problem.

Escaping with Credit Cards

Credit cards are another good method of getting cash quickly. International cards, such as Visa and Mastercard, can be used to draw cash advances at member banks all over the world. American Express has offices worldwide where cardholders can draw, depending on their credit limit, as much as $1,000 (up to $200 in local currency and up to $800 in traveler's checks).

 **Don't send bank transfers blind. Pick the bank where you want the money sent first. Find out what bank they deal with in the U.S., and then wire specific routing details back to your own bank.**

Credit cards can be used for purchases as well as cash advances, of course, and they provide a nice backup in emergencies. Used with care (it's easy to overextend if you don't keep good records), they can relieve you of having to carry large amounts of cash.

The biggest problem with them is paying for the charges to avoid the high interest. With the inevitable delays that occur in the mail-forwarding process, it takes some careful planning to make payments on time. One solution is to authorize your bank to automatically pay the bill each month. Some brokerage firms also will do this by deducting the amount from interest and dividends earned, or by selling enough securities to cover the charges.

Another method was suggested by Bill and Alma Russell, who cruised the Bahamas aboard their 30-foot sloop *Heron*. Before leaving, Alma made a note of the billing date for each card they carried.

During the cruise, she saved all receipts and kept a record of purchases and advances. The companies they dealt with agreed to accept payments without being accompanied by the computerized billing card. So, after the closing date each month, Alma totaled up the charges and sent off a check. When the mail eventually caught up to them, she compared the bills with the payments to make sure everything was correct. If you choose this method, make arrangements—in writing—before setting out. And be sure to write the account number on each check before mailing it.

Unraveling Exchange Rates

While opinions vary on strategies for getting the best rate of exchange, one point everyone agrees on is that generally you will lose some money in every currency exchange. Lin Pardey estimates she spent $70 to $80 a year in exchange rates and charges. She recommends not changing money the first day in a new port, but checking around with other travelers and at banks and shops to find out who offers the best rates. Sy Carkhuff found that in most places he got better rates at local stores than at banks.

Earl Hinz, on the other hand, would only deal with banks during his South Pacific cruises. He said they gave the best rates, especially on traveler's checks, and also said banks are the safest place to convert money. How would you recognize counterfeit foreign currency, he asks.

 Credit cards are an excellent way to get cash away from home and nice to have in an emergency. But beware high interest charges levied because of mail-forwarding delays.

Don't try to save money by converting on the black market. Many countries impose heavy fines and even jail sentences for illegal exchanges. Lin Pardey said they did do it on a few occasions, but only where the penalty for a first-time offense was nothing more than a warning. Only change money where the rates are posted and where you can get a receipt.

Before having money wired, find out both the exchange rate and any bank charges for converting from U.S. dollars. Then decide whether it's better to have your bank send U.S. or local currency. Banks generally charge 1%–2% for each foreign exchange, but sometimes as much as 4%.

Exchange rates on traveler's checks are often 2% better than what is offered on credit card advances.

Since you are likely to lose money on every transaction, it makes sense to exchange only what's necessary. Not only will you pay when you convert from U.S. to local currency, but you pay again to change back to U.S. dollars before heading on to another country.

To plan ahead, the best place to find out foreign exchange rates is at an international bank. Small local banks will sometimes, but not always, have the information you want, but an international bank always will.

It helps to know currency regulations, too. Wayne Carpenter once cashed a $1,000 check in Costa Rica and discovered to his surprise that, by national law, he was only allowed to receive $300 in U.S. currency. The rest had to be in colones. The transaction was officially entered in his passport.

There are several places to obtain currency regulations of countries you plan to visit. An international bank with offices in those countries will know of any restrictions. Travel agents are usually a wealth of information. Besides knowing currency regulations and limitations on duty-free purchases, they often have booklets and brochures that are free for the asking.

Cruising guides, written by and for sailing people, often contain information about currency restrictions and money changing. I've always found that cruising guides—if they existed for an area I planned to visit—were a worthwhile investment. The same can be said for any number of travel guides available at most good bookstores.

 Check out penalties for black market currency exchanges before taking the risk. The safest rule is to change money only where rates are posted and receipts given.

And let's not neglect governments (ours or theirs). U.S. Customs will tell you about money regulations as well as restrictions on bringing goods back into the States, required immunization shots, and restrictions on pets and plants. Check your telephone directory for the nearest customs office (listed as a division of the U.S. Treasury Department).

Another source of information is the government of the country you're visiting. Most countries have embassies in Washington, D.C. that you can write or call. Many have consulates, especially in large cities. A response may take a while, but sometimes the result is a pleasant surprise. When I wrote to the Greek Embassy, almost two months passed before anyone replied. But in addition to answering my questions, they sent along a beautiful four-color book about traveling in Greece.

Addresses and phone numbers for all foreign embassies can be found at most local libraries. Ask for a U.S. Government publication called the *Washington Information Directory*. The book also gives the phone number of the U.S. State Department office that is assigned to keep track of political, cultural and economic developments of each particular country.

Personal Identification

For any transaction you will need plenty of identification. Whether you're receiving a money transfer or cashing a check, take along as much as possible: a passport, driver's license, ship's papers, credit cards, radio operator's license, anything that looks official and has your name on it or, even better, your picture.

By far the best form of identification is a passport, even for traveling in the United States. Banks and shops in small towns will accept a U.S. passport more readily than an out-of-state driver's license.

When having money sent by any means (check, transfer, money order or whatever), have it made out exactly as your name appears on your passport. A passport for Robert Smith and a check make out to Bob Smith could create confusion and needless delay in a foreign bank where the manager doesn't understand American nicknames. If a check is made out to two people, be sure it says "or" between the names so either one can cash it.

 **Make sure to have checks, money orders, etc. made out to you** *exactly* **as your name appears on your major forms of personal identification.**

CHAPTER EIGHT

Getting News From Afar

No news isn't always good news

It's wonderful to sit an anchor in a secluded cove, alone except for the gentle calling of shore birds and an occasional fish breaking the calm surface of pale blue water. Nothing around but white sandy beaches and swaying palm trees. Nothing to do but swim and snorkel and stroll along the beach looking for shells.

Equally wonderful is to come to a new city, locate the post office, and discover there's a mail package waiting with newsy letters from home, cards from new friends met along the way and old friends left far astern, a bank statement and business correspondence. It will make you feel closer to loved ones while at the same time emphasizing the distance between you.

Communication with the world "back there," usually by mail but sometimes by phone, isn't always just for fun. There may be an elderly parent you need to keep tabs on, or a business associate who's running the store in your absence. And you will find the farther you get from home the more important getting mail becomes.

Choosing a Forwarding Agent

The most important factor in deciding who will handle mail is whether or not they are *reliable*. Ninety-nine percent of the time this rules out friends. No matter how close a friend they are or how well-intentioned at the start, sooner or later they will get tired of the work involved, tired of the responsibility, or tired of the occasional expense if postage isn't reimbursed promptly. If they are young and mobile they could move, leaving you to find a new agent (and possibly a new address) from thousands of miles away. They could get divorced, or get sick and spend a month in the hospital. It's best to keep a friend as just that: a friend, not a forwarding agent.

Maybe blood really is thicker than water, because quite a few voyaging sailors successfully use family members. More often than not, it's Mom. A relative will be more sympathetic and more understanding than a friend about the importance of your mail. An older family member, particularly a parent, is likely to be settled into a stable lifestyle and may well enjoy sharing in the escape vicariously by acting as a forwarding agent. It's a good way for them to know that no matter where you roam you *will* stay in touch.

The best plan, however, is to pay someone to perform the service. If you do, hire a professional. It is not that expensive, and it means that the agent views it as a job, not as a favor that becomes an imposition. If an attorney or accountant is already handling other business matters, it should be a simple matter to include mail forwarding, as well.

A secretarial service in your home town is a good choice. I have had quotes ranging from $15 a month to as high as $50 a month, so do some checking first. They could do other tasks as well, such as making bank deposits and paying bills on time.

There are a number of mail forwarding services. See Table 1 for a list of services and their addresses. Most of them are excellent. Mail-forwarding is their only business, they are familiar with postage and shipping world-wide and—most importantly—they understand the special needs of someone who travels a great deal.

I have used the same service—MCCA, Inc. in Estes Park, Colorado

---

TABLE 1   **MAIL FORWARDING SERVICES**

AIMS
  Box 1329
  Ontario, CA 91761
	NATO
	  Box 1418
	  Sarasota, FL 33578

Bellevue Avenue Executive Mailboxes
  38 Bellevue Avenue
  Newport, RI 02840
  (401) 849-2200
	TOMA
	  Box 2010
	  Sparks, NV 39431

Home Base
  P.O. Box 226
  Long Beach, NY 11561
	TRA
	  710 W. Main
	  Arlington, TX 76013
	  (817) 261-6072

The Mail Bag
  P.O. Box 6592
  Anaheim, CA 92306
	Urban Mail Box Service
	  111 E. Second St.
	  Perrysburg, OH 43551

MCCA, Inc.
  P.O. Box 2870
  Estes Park, CO 80517
  (800) 525-5304	

—for more than four years now and have never had a problem. MCCA's cost and operating procedures are typical of most services. MCCA costs $50 to join. That includes a $30 annual fee plus a $20 postage deposit. When the postage account gets low, they send a bill for another deposit.

 **You will find the farther you get from home the more important getting mail becomes.**

MCCA will accept packages from United Parcel Service (UPS), then hold them until they receive forwarding instructions. Many companies automatically ship UPS, and you have no way of knowing if they are shipping promptly, back ordering or twiddling their thumbs. Using a forwarding service will prevent getting hung up in port wondering when the package will arrive. You can keep cruising until you know for sure the service has received it.

The major reason I chose MCCA over the others is its toll-free 800 number that can be called 24 hours a day from anywhere in the continental United States. For coastal cruising, it virtually cut in half the turn-around time for receiving mail. Outside the U.S. or in Hawaii, of course, written instructions must be sent, or you must bear the cost of telephoning.

Additionally, MCCA will take telephone messages and include the messages when they send a mail packet. The charge is $1.00 a message, deducted from the postage account. Not all services offer this, so be sure to check if it is important to you.

Mail Drops that Work

General delivery works well in the United States. A post office will hold mail for 10 to 15 days (it varies from one town to the next). Not *all* post offices will accept general delivery mail, however. It's generally only the main post office in town and not the branch office. Cruising guides (such as the *Waterway Guide* for the east coast) often will list mail drops for the area covered, and even give the distance from the harbor to the post office.

Outside the U.S., general delivery is chancy at best. Sy Carkhuff said he lost quite a bit of mail using general delivery. Even though post offices everywhere supposedly return mail to the sender if it's not picked up, Sy says it never happened. The mail just disappeared. He discovered that banks in foreign countries are very reliable mail drops (he used Barclays Bank most often).

Wayne Carpenter remembers having a $1,000 cashier's check mailed to him c/o general delivery at the post office at Playa el Cocos in Costa Rica. When they made port, Wayne was directed to a broken-down shack on the beach. The "post office" was an unlocked, unattended building with a stack of mail just inside a teller's window. He reached in, thumbed through the mail and extracted his check. It had been sitting there a week.

The following are some good places to have mail forwarded to:

- Yacht clubs
- Marinas/hotels
- International banks
- American Express offices
- Port Captains
- Make a friend in town and use their address.

Mailing Mechanics

Several months before leaving, start giving close attention to every piece of paper that arrives in the mailbox. Decide if it's really necessary to continue receiving it while you're away, and cancel it if it isn't. A marine hardware catalog? Maybe. A Horchow catalog? I doubt it! Remember *you* are now paying the postage to have all that junk mail follow you around the world.

Have mail packets sent "first class" or "priority" in the United States and air mail elsewhere. Any other way just takes too long. The exception is magazines, catalogs and other bulky or heavy items that are low priority. Have them held until you know you will be someplace for a couple of months, them have them sent "book rate" or surface mail. And you can bet it's a slow boat to China, Tahiti or Australia.

If you're cruising, envelopes should bear your name, the boat's name and mark in the lower corner "Hold for Arrival." Envelopes and packages mailed at the same time will seldom *arrive* at the same time. Whenever your agent sends more than one bundle, they should mark *each* one: "#1 of 2," "#2 of 2," etc. Otherwise, you could pick up mail, sail away and never know more mail arrived three days later.

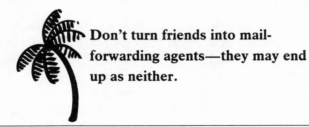

Don't turn friends into mail-forwarding agents—they may end up as neither.

Just like cashing a check, take along plenty of identification when picking up mail. Instruct your agent to write out your name exactly as it appears on your passport, licenses and other papers.

Phoning from Afar

Mail takes a long time, and occasions will come up when faster communication is needed. Almost every country in the world has telephone service. It may be marginal in some areas, but it's still the fastest way of getting in touch.

A good plan for someone who knows they will be making a lot of calls is to carry a telephone credit card, available from any telephone company. There is no charge for the card, but there must be an in-service telephone somewhere that charges can be billed to. Unless you have a home or business phone that will remain in service while you're voyaging, other arrangements will need to be made. It might be possible to bill charges to your attorney's phone, or to your accountant, forwarding agent, or even a relative. Careful records should be kept to keep your calls separate from the rest.

For a short escape, it is possible to get vacation service. The phone is temporarily disconnected and the charge is one-half the normal monthly rate. This allows you to keep the same phone number and continue using the credit card. Pacific Telephone will extend vacation service for up to eight months, and charges $22 to reconnect.

Credit cards carry two numbers. The domestic number is used in the United States and for calls to the U.S. from Canada, Bermuda, the Bahamas and most of the Caribbean. The international number is used to call back to the United States from other countries that honor the card. It can be used in 93 countries around the world. Information on rates and restrictions for different countries can be obtained by calling International Information toll-free: 1-800-874-4000. International calls made with the credit card are billed in U.S. currency at the U.S. rate.

Without a credit card, calls can be made by calling collect, by plunking a bag full of coins into a phone booth and, in some places, through offices similar to Western Union.

If you seldom make a phone call, or always call the same person, it may be easiest to call collect. Make arrangements before leaving to be sure it's acceptable, and to assure the other party they will be reimbursed. During the seven years I cruised without a telephone credit card (I now have one), I called my father collect at least twice a month. He insisted on it, and it reassured me that he was still in good health and all was well at home. Virtually all of my other correspondence was strictly by mail.

Making a long distance phone call from a pay phone (other than calling collect) is always a pain. It requires getting stacks of change, dropping them one by one into the slot and then hoping like crazy the phone won't devour them if no one answers at the other end. Calling person to person is more expensive than direct dialing, but at least it doesn't run the risk of being put on hold until your money runs out or finding out your party isn't in and having to pay for the call, anyway. Most frustrating of all is spending four or five dollars (or more) only to get one of those recording machines saying, "Leave your number and I'll return your call" when your only "number" is a phone booth.

Almost all countries have companies similar to our Western Union where telegrams and night letters can be sent. Night letters should arrive by the following day and cost less than a straight telegram.

Sometimes these offices will include a tele-communications division with private booths where telephone calls can be made. The calls are placed by an operator there, and paid for in cash.

 **The best mail forwarders are the professional services. They know shipping & postage world-wide and they understand the special needs of travelers.**

Pay phones outside the U.S. aren't always as reliable as what we're used to. I remember going to a total of seven different phone booths in Nassau, Bahamas. Not one of them worked. Finally I was directed to a big hotel across from the marina, where two rooms were provided, each containing several telephones. After paying the desk clerk one dollar in U.S. currency, I stood in line for two hours, then made my call (to the entertainment of everyone else in line). But at least the call got through, and as a bonus I met half the yachties visiting Nassau. It turned out to be a great meeting place.

Hotels always are a good bet for finding a usable telephone, and so are yacht clubs. Sometimes marinas will allow the use of their inside phone, but more often you'll be directed to the pay phones outside. Another place to try is an American embassy or consulate office.

Communicating by Radio

VHF/FM RADIO

With a VHF (very high frequency) radio, calls can be made from ship-to-ship, from ship-to-shore, shore-to-shore and to any telephone by going through a marine or land operator.

VHF is essentially line-of-sight, and antenna height is the major factor in determining the range. As a general rule of thumb, the formula is $1.4 \sqrt{H}$, with H being the height above the water (or land) in feet. Under rare conditions, transmissions have been picked up as far away as 200 miles, but 35 miles is more common.

VHF radios are not expensive and most boats, both pleasure and commercial, are equipped with them, as are many trucks, taxis and other land-based vehicles. They range in price from around $300 for a small 12-channel set useful for local voyaging up to as much as $2,000 for a fully synthesized unit with all U.S. and international channels. There's a wide variety in between. Virtually all new VHF/FM radios are synthesized, i.e., they can receive all the channels shown on their dial. The old crystal sets required purchasing a separate crystal for each channel desired.

The Federal Communications Commission (FCC) has strict rules governing use of VHF radio. Any time the radio is on and not in active use, channel 16—the distress channel—must be monitored. Additionally, channel 16 is the "calling" channel. All calls must originate on channel 16 before switching to the appropriate working channel. Table 2 lists the marine channels assigned to pleasure boats, and

TABLE 2   **VHF CHANNELS FOR PLEASURE BOATS**

Channel	Usage
16	A required channel. Distress, safety and calling
06	A required channel. Ship-to-ship safety communications
09	Only channel assigned for communications between commercial and non-commercial vessels
12	Port operations, traffic advisory
13	Used for safety when maneuvering in close quarters. Monitored by tugs, barges and dredges in waterways. Restricted to "bridge to bridge" (meaning a vessel's control station)
14	Port operations, for communicating with bridge and lock tenders
22A	Non-distress communications with United States Coast Guard
24, 25, 26, 27, 28	Marine Operator (26 and 28 are preferred)
68, 69	Non-commercial ship-to-ship and ship-to-shore (yacht clubs, marinas, etc.); 68 is preferred
70, 72	Non-commercial ship-to-ship (70 is preferred)
71, 78	Non-commercial ship-to-ship and ship-to-shore
WX-1, WX-2, WX-3	Weather broadcasts

describes their intended use. These channels are for radio use in the United States. Some of them will be different in foreign countries. In Canadian waters, for instance, non-commercial ship-to-ship calls can be made on channel 8 but not on 70 or 72. It's another good reason for having a synthesized radio instead of crystal.

On land, the FCC is far stricter in its VHF regulations. Specific businesses will be assigned certain frequencies. Most general communications go through mobile radiotelephone operators through a network of repeater stations that extend the usual 20–40 mile range of the VHF. Those wishing to communicate directly with a companion vehicle or other radio station would be much better off using Citizen's Band (CB) radio or ham radio (more on this later in this chapter).

Aside from distress and safety calls, ship-to-ship calls are limited to "operational" communications. According to the FCC, operational calls fall into three categories:

- NAVIGATION—Anything relating to the actual piloting of the boat.
- MOVEMENT—Matters relating to *future* movements of the boat; calling another boat to find out if the anchorage area is crowded or to arrange a rendezvous, for instance.
- MANAGEMENT—Calls relating to boat repairs, getting dockage, fuel, water, etc.

Calls of a personal or "social" nature between boats are forbidden, although anyone who has ever listened to the Sunday afternoon chit-chat on the radio knows how often this is abused. The exception to these rules is ship-to-shore calls placed through the Marine Operator. They may be of a personal or social nature. You *can* call Grandma and wish her a happy birthday.

Outside the U.S., general delivery is chancy. Try making a friend in the town you're in and using their address.

Billing procedures for ship-to-shore and shore-to-shore calls vary from one area to the next. Sometimes calls can be made collect, sometimes billed to your home or business phone or telephone credit card, and other times the operator will just ask for your mailing/billing address.

For cruising in the United States, it's a good idea to get a special credit card with a marine identification number, called a MIN card. The card is issued by the telephone company's mobile marine division and can only be used with the ship's radio (calls made from a phone on shore cannot be charged to it). All the phone company requires is the boat's name and registration number, the radio's call sign, and the owner's name and billing address. There is no charge for the card, no monthly fee and it can be used anywhere in the U.S. and in parts of Canada. A bill is only sent when the card is used to place a call. Unlike a regular telephone credit card, you do *not* have to have an in-service telephone ashore.

To legally operate a VHF radio, the following are required:

- A station license, posted near the radio.
- A restricted Radiotelephone Operator Permit, posted near the radio or carried with you.
- A station log, kept up-to-date.
- A current copy of the FCC VHF Rules and Regulations.

The station license and operator permit can be obtained from:

Federal Communications Commission
P.O. Box 1040
Gettysburg, PA 17325

For the station license, request FCC Form 506, and for the operator permit, FCC Form 753. In January 1977, the FCC suspended license and permit fees, so there is no charge.

The rules and regulations are included in simplified form in a 30-page book called "How to Use Your VHF Marine Radio: FCC Rules for Recreational Boaters, Part 83, Subpart CC." Order it from:

Superintendent of Documents
U.S. Government Printing Office
Washington, D.C. 20402

or, on the west coast, from:

> Government Printing Office
> Branch Bookstore No. 10
> ARCO Plaza, Level C
> 505 Flower St.
> Los Angeles, CA 90071

The cost is $3.75, including tax and shipping. If ordering from Washington, D.C., include the stock number: 004-000-00-386-1.

SINGLE SIDEBAND (SSB) RADIO

An MF-HF (medium and high frequencies) single sideband radio can only be installed if the boat is already equipped with a VHF/FM radio *and* if the owner can show that he or she will be cruising further offshore than the short-range VHF radio can reach. Communications are similar to VHF but with a much longer range. If the calling distance is fairly short, VHF *must* be tried first before the SSB set can be used. SSB can be installed on a land vehicle but, again, only with FCC permission.

Certain frequencies have been assigned in different bands, usually near 2, 4, 6, 8, 12, 16 and 22 MHz. The MF frequency for safety, distress and calling is 2182 kHz and it must be installed in every SSB radio. Other frequencies are used for Coast Guard communication and as ship-to-ship channels.

 **Before leaving, start scrutinizing every piece of incoming mail. If you don't want to pay postage to send it halfway around the world, cancel it.**

Ship-to-shore calls through the marine operator are assigned to two services:

- COASTAL SERVICE—Uses the 2 and 4 MHz bands. There are stations in 30 major United States shipping ports and a large number of major foreign ports. The range is about 200 miles on 2 MHz and several times greater at night on 4 MHz.
- HIGH-SEAS SERVICE—Uses frequencies in the 4, 8, 12 and 16 MHz bands.

An SSB radio is not inexpensive, with prices starting at about $2,000 and going all the way up to $10,000. Licensing requirements are the same as for a VHF. While a VHF can be installed by a boat owner, a single sideband installation must be done by a licensed technician.

AMATEUR (HAM) RADIO

The time spent in obtaining a ham radio license is a worthwhile investment for the offshore cruiser or anyone voyaging away from civilization. With the right equipment and license, a ham operator can, quite literally, be in touch with the entire world. In any kind of emergency, from medical to storm damage, the network of ham operators can be a lifeline to expert advice or rescue by helicopter.

While amateur radio cannot be used for any commercial purpose, there are no time restrictions on length of conversations. Worldwide "nets," including ones in the Pacific, Caribbean and Atlantic, go on the air at set times and on specific frequencies to share information and relay messages from friends and families back home. From just about anywhere, phone calls can be patched through back to the States. See Table 3 for a list of the existing maritime mobile nets. While the chart lists all of the major nets, there are always small local nets scattered around familiar only to local ham operators.

Unlike other types of non-commercial radio, a ham license involves much more than a formal request. Operators must pass tests on amateur radio theory and Morse Code. Many balk at the thought of learning code, but it's just a matter of practice, practice, practice, and it *is* important. Morse Code (carrier wave—CW—transmission) can almost always cut through interference and noise when voice transmission would get lost in the garble. And the three-letter "Q" signals are a universal language, allowing communication with other hams regardless of their native tongue.

| TABLE 3 **MARITIME MOBILE NETS** | | | | | | | |
| Chart courtesy of Gordon West. | | | | | | | |

Meters	Band Name	kHz	Zulu	Ends	PST	PDT	Days
15	Inter-American Net	21,415	2030	0	1230	1330	
15	Int'l Maritime Net	21,404	2200	2300	1400	1500	Mon/Fri
20	Seafarers/Maritime Service Net	14,313	200	500	1800	1900	
20	DDD Net-Pacific for Canadians	14,115	400	0	2000	2100	Daily
20	Maritime emergency	14,310	400	1600	800	1900	
20	Pacific Maritime	14,313	500	600	2300	2400	Daily
20	Marianas-Guam	14,310	700	800	2300	2400	Daily
20	So. Pacific	14,315	800	0	0	100	
20	Gunkholers Net-Tulagi	14,328	1000	0	300	200	
20	North Net	14,345	1445	0	745	745	Daily
20	Marquesas	14,340	1545	0	745	845	
20	Atlanta	14,313	1600	1700	800	900	
20	Cal-Hawaii	14,340	1630	0	830	930	
20	DDD Net-Pacific for Canadians	14,115	1730	0	930	1030	Mon/Fri
20	Chaplin Robinson	14,313	1800	2300	1000	1100	Daily
20	Manana	14,340	1900	0	1100	1200	Mon/Sat
20	East Coast Waterway	14,290	2130	0	1330	1430	M-W-F
20	Calif to So. Pac.	14,285	2300	2310	1500	1600	Mon
20	Calif. to Caribbean	14,285	2310	2320	1510	1620	Mon
40	Carib Net	7158	0	0	1600	1700	
40	East Coast Waterway	7268	1330	0	530	630	Daily
40	Baja Net to LaPaz	7235	1600	1630	800	900	Daily
40	Maritime Mobile	7245	1600	0	800	900	
40	WESCARS	7255	1700	0	900	1000	Daily
40	Serarpe Net Admirals	7280	1730	0	930	1030	Sun
40	Shamaru/Smitty Hawaii Net	7285	1900	0	1100	1200	
40	West Coast Admirals	7190	2230	2300	1430	1530	Daily
75	So. Pacific	3815	715	0	2315	15	
75	East Coast Waterway	3968	1345	0	545	645	Daily

A "novice" license requires sending and receiving code at five words a minute and passing a written test on basic radio theory, rules and operating procedures. A novice is not allowed to use voice transmission, only code on a limited number of frequencies.

The "general class" license permits worldwide voice transmission as well as code. The test includes more advanced electronics theory and a code speed of 13 words a minute. A "technician class" license allows voice transmission, but only on limited frequencies. It can be useful for coastal cruisers who have a hand-held radio with two and six-meter bands ($200–$250). Repeaters are located along the coast to extend the range of these radios. The written test for the technician and general licenses is the same, but only five words a minute code speed is required for a technician license.

Advanced and extra licenses require even more knowledge and higher code speeds, but the privileges are greater, too. For long-distance cruisers, a general class license is recommended as a minimum.

Classes are frequently offered by local radio clubs and community colleges. Taz and I enrolled in a nine-week ham radio class sponsored by his yacht club that cost us $50 each. The course helped us pass the technician class exam. Continued practice will get us to the 13 words a minute for a general license.

I found the structure and discipline of attending weekly classes extremely helpful, but many people do it on their own. For a catalog and list of study materials and information on how to get started, write:

"I Want to be a Ham"
Ham Radio Horizons
Greenville, New Hampshire 03048

Or call Ham Radio Horizons' toll-free number: 1-800-258-5353.

 **Among the place you'll always find a telephone in working order are good hotels, yacht clubs, U.S. embassies and U.S. consulate offices.**

A ham radio setup suitable for offshore cruising can run from $1,000–$2,000, although used equipment can sometimes be found by checking with local clubs. It may seem expensive, but it is the best form of mobile radio communication.

CHAPTER NINE

Insuring the Escape Machine

Ultimately, it's mind over matter

To insure or not to insure, that is the question, and it's a big one. Sy Carkhuff, who lectured extensively around the country after he and Vicki completed their sailing circumnavigation, estimates that of the hundreds of cruising people he met and talked with while lecturing as well as cruising, only about 35% carried boat insurance. Sy and Vicki did carry insurance for their 40-foot sloop *Resolve*, at a cost of $300 a month. That's a whopping $3,600 a year.

In December of 1982 a disastrous storm screamed its way through Cabo San Lucas in Baja, California. Out of 49 anchored boats, 23 were swept ashore. W. David Cookingham, a marine surveyor from San Diego who spent five days in Cabo San Lucas after the storm, said only half the boats lost were insured.

I'm always amazed at the ability of so many cruising people to bounce back after losing their boats. After the Baja storm, many of the wrecked boats were hauled off the beach, extensively repaired and are now cruising again. Others salvaged as much as they could and are hard at work building new boats.

People's attitudes toward insurance often change when they decide to escape in expensive vehicles—boats, campers, RVs, etc. I've heard quite a few say that they simply cannot afford the insurance and they are not about to allow the lack of it keep them from experiencing the adventure of a lifetime. Sailors who make such statements usually have a great deal of local and coastal cruising experience and who thus have the confidence to handle their boats—and themselves—in just about any situation.

Bob and Shearlean Duke, both experienced sailors, are about to set off for extended cruising in their 35-foot cutter. The first year they will cruise Mexico and the Sea of Cortez, and they *will* carry insurance. But only for the first year. Bob says insurance in Mexico is affordable, and adds you are more likely to make mistakes during the first "shakedown" year of cruising. When the Dukes leave Mexico for more distant ports, they will carry no insurance.

The length of the escape—both in time and distance—seems to be the major factor in determining whether to insure the escape vehicle. Many more boats that cruise in home waters, for example, carry insurance. It is affordable near home, whereas the cost for long-distance insurance is usually prohibitive. Also, a great many vehicles used near home are financed, and thus are required to carry insurance. Since insurance for "local" cruising is the most common, let's look at that first.

The Basics of Yacht Insurance

A yacht insurance policy is generally separated into two distinct categories: the boat and its equipment and liability. Most companies will write a policy just for hull insurance (the expensive part) with no liability coverage (the inexpensive part). It is just about impossible, however, to buy boat liability insurance without also buying hull insurance.

Occasionally hull insurance is written on the basis of "named peril" —that is, the boat is only covered if it is lost or damaged as a result of dangers specifically spelled out in the policy. The better type of coverage, and the more common one, is called "all risk." With all risk, the boat is insured against direct physical loss or damage from an accidental cause. The exclusions are listed, instead of the causes. Some typical exclusions are:

- Any loss resulting from normal wear and tear, gradual deterioration, mechanical breakdown, rot, corrosion or weathering.
- Any loss caused by vermin or marine life.
- Any loss caused by ice or freezing.
- Any loss or damage caused intentionally by a person insured under the policy.
- Loss or damage as a result of war, including undeclared war, civil war, insurrection, rebellion or revolution. Whew!
- Any loss caused by radioactive contamination.

Coverage of an insured boat generally includes the hull, spars, sails, machinery, outboard motors, furniture, usually a dinghy that's used as a tender, and equipment that is considered normal for the operation and maintenance of the boat. Personal items, such as televisions, cameras, scuba gear, portable radios, etc., are often included, but only up to a specified limit. Live-aboards who have sold their house and furniture and who no longer have a "homeowner's policy" might want to consider having the "personal effects" portion of their yacht policy increased substantially.

The liability portion of a marine insurance policy (called "P&I"— protection and indemnity) provides coverage against bodily injury for the insured, his family and guests. P&I coverage is not provided for a paid captain or crew. This must be covered under a separate policy. Liability also covers property damage caused by the insured, his family and guests. This includes such things as running into another boat or ramming a dock, piling or buoy. Removing or disposing of the insured boat also is covered, as long as such removal is required by law. Liability is most often written for a $300,000 limit, although it can vary anywhere from $25,000 to $500,000 or more.

P&I covers bodily injury to anyone working on the boat (repairmen, mechanics) under the Federal Longshoremen's and Harbor Workers' Compensation Act.

 **Many people who want to take off in their expensive escape machines say they simply can't afford insurance. But that doesn't always stop them from going on an adventure of a lifetime.**

Medical insurance usually is included without an additional premium. This covers medical accidents for the insured, his family and guests, but does not cover hired crew or workers, and the limits are usually low—from $1,000 to $5,000.

Yacht policies always are written for a specific "navigational limit." If you take the boat outside the limits, you are no longer insured. In Southern California, for example, policies are written for "Pacific coastal waters and tributaries not north of Point Conception, California, nor south of Rio Santo Tomas, Mexico." East coast limitations are typically Eastport, Maine, to Cedar Keys, Florida. Seasonal limits are a factor, too. If a boat will be in Mexico during the chubasco season and the owner can even get insurance, he will be told in which harbors he must remain to stay insured.

"Riders" can be purchased at an additional premium to extend coverage beyond normal limits. A typical rider for the east coast extends insurance to the Bahamas.

Many insurance companies give discounts for such things as a diesel engine, for certain types of safety or electronic gear aboard, or for completing a U.S. Power Squadron or Coast Guard Auxiliary safe boat handling course.

Cost of yacht insurance varies widely, and much is left to the discretion and judgment of the broker. Some of the factors that can influence the cost of boat insurance are:

- Condition of the boat, based on a recent (within 12 months) survey.
- Hull material, whether fiberglass, wood, steel, aluminum or ferro-cement.
- Age of the boat. Some companies won't insure a boat that's more than 15 or 20 years old.
- Safety and navigation equipment carried aboard.
- Age, sailing abilities and experience of skipper and crew.
- The amount of deductible.
- Whether the boat has a gasoline or diesel auxiliary.
- Completion of a piloting or seamanship course sponsored by the U.S. Power Squadron or Coast Guard Auxiliary.

Some companies offer a percentage discount for each loss-free year. The part of the country in which you live and cruise makes a difference, too. According to Boat Owners Association of the U.S. (BOAT/US), insurance is more costly east than west. The following is a list of geographic areas, beginning with the most expensive area down to the least expensive:

- Gulf of Mexico
- Florida's east coast
- The rest of the Atlantic coast (with higher rates in the north Atlantic)
- Chesapeake Bay and the Great Lakes
- Pacific coast, and inland lakes and rivers

Although no rules exist for figuring insurance costs, the following are some examples of what people are now paying:

- A 1957 40-foot ketch, for Southern California area:
  Hull: $58,000; P&I: $300,000; Medical: $5,000
  Personal effects: $250; Deductible on the hull: $1,160; Total premium: $819/year.

- A 1977 30-foot fiberglass sloop, for Southern California area:
  Hull: $34,000; P&I: $300,000; Medical: $1,000
  Personal effects: $500; Deductible on the hull: $640; Total premium: $351/year.

- A 1976 32-foot fiberglass sloop, for all of east coast of U.S. and Bahamas:
  Hull: $60,000; Deductible on the hull: $1,500; Total premium: $1,030/year.

- A 1982 30-foot fiberglass sloop, for east coast of U.S.
  Hull: $14,000; P&I: $300,000; Medical: $3,000; Deductible on the hull: $280; Total premium: $320/year.

Insurance for An Extended Cruising Escape

Once you decide to leave home waters, the rates go up and so do the requirements that must be met by boat and crew. American companies won't write for "round the world" passages. They only will insure for certain areas. BOAT/US for instance, will write extended cruising coverage only to Bermuda, the Caribbean, Central America and the Panama Canal—and then only for long-range trawlers or sailboats larger than 35 feet and less than 15 years old.

Some companies will insure for a particular destination but will impose a time limit. National American will insure boats going to Hawaii, but will cancel the insurance if the boat remains in Hawaiian waters for more than a year. This is because of the scarcity of safe Hawaiian harbors and the weather that sometimes wreaks havoc in the islands—as evidenced by Hurricane Iwa in 1982. The longer a boat stays there, the higher its chances of getting caught in a storm.

Another point to check: Be sure the coverage includes local cruising (within a 100-mile radius, perhaps) once the specified destination is reached. Depending on the wording in the policy, you could sail to a major port only to discover that you can't leave until time to return home. It's important to note that once you leave the navigational limits of your policy, it is no longer valid, even if you then return to "protected" waters.

Even more than with local cruising, the cost of insuring a boat for extended cruising is largely a matter of your broker's judgment. He, the underwriter (insurance company), and the surveyor don't just settle rates for the premium, they first decide whether they even will insure the boat. The following are some of the points that could influence their decision:

- Number of people aboard, and how much offshore experience each has. Many companies want four adults on the boat, all with offshore experience. A boat operated by "Mom and Pop" isn't music to an underwriter's ears.
- Ability and experience of the skipper. Usually a resume is requested, listing previous cruises, types of boats owned or skippered in the past, age, health, and how long he or she has been sailing, particularly offshore.
- Skills and experience of the navigator. It's often preferred that two people on board know celestial navigation, and are able to operate all of the boat's electronic equipment.
- Whether or not someone aboard has previously cruised in the intended area.

 **Boat insurance policies always contain limits of permitted navigation. Before heading for tropic seas, check whether your policy will remain in force.**

The boat and its equipment will be scrutinized just as carefully as the crew. In almost every instance, a "trip" survey (a condition and valuation survey) will be required. Bob Duke, a marine surveyor in California who frequently does trip surveys, said trip surveys are quite different from general surveys done for local insurance or financing.

He says it is a general survey *plus*. For instance, in a general survey he simply checks the fresh water system to make sure it works. For local sailing, water is pretty easy to come by. But for long distance cruising he checks the system very carefully, determining if the tanks are of adequate capacity; if they are structurally sound and well secured; if the hoses are securely clamped; and if there's a way to get water from the tanks should the pumps fail.

According to Bob, among the items necessary to pass a trip survey are:

- Gear and equipment properly stowed for violent motion in a seaway.
- Sufficient sea berths.
- Enough fire extinguishers for fighting more than one fire.
- Life jackets and safety equipment—including a life raft—large enough for the entire crew.
- A complete medical kit and first aid manual.
- An autopilot or wine vane, particularly if the crew is short-handed.
- A recently adjusted (preferably by a professional) compass.
- A well-running engine, including adequate spares, extra oil, transmision fluid, etc.
- Operating manuals for all equipment on board.
- Fuel tanks and the fuel system in good condition.
- Strong batteries
- Ventilators that can be closed and made watertight
- Rigging and sails in good condition and spare rigging, fittings, etc.
- Storm sails.
- Adequate ground tackle, including a storm anchor.
- Ports and windows that can be secured and protected from boarding seas.
- Cockpit drains and scuppers able to quickly drain away a boarding sea.
- Adequate bilge pumps, both electric and manual.
- A sound hull, suitable for the proposed cruise.

The surveyor or underwriter also will want to see a complete list of all charts, coast pilots and sailing directions. And, finally, the underwriter will want to have a trip itinerary that includes the proposed cruising area, intended ports of call and approximate dates for the trip.

The owner pays for the trip survey. It can run from $2.75 to $4.00 a foot for a fiberglass boat. Bob Duke says wood, steel or aluminum boats require more work to survey and the charges will range from $3.50 to $5.50 a foot.

Here's a statement that should come as no surprise: Insurance rates for extended cruising coverage vary widely, influenced by the factors we've just discussed as well as the opinions of the surveyor, broker and underwriter. Additionally, a higher deductible will be required. One jovial broker told me rates really are set "by shooting craps."

Typically, rates start at about 1.25% of the hull value, and go up from there, with a minimum deductible of 3%. The rate can be held in the lower ranges by an owner willing to accept a higher deductible. But keep in mind what Mike Sciulla at BOAT/US told me. "The deductible represents the first dollar of every loss. Don't accept a deductible higher than your bank account or you may find yourself in a foreign port without the financial wherewithal to make repairs."

For an example, let's look at that 1977 30-foot fiberglass sloop valued at $34,000, and insured for local cruising at an annual premium of $351 with a $640 deductible. Assume the owner met all the requirements and was able to get insurance for a year's cruise outside his home waters. At a rate of 1.25% of hull value and a 3% deductible, his premium would increase to $425 with a deductible of $1,020.

 **The golden rule for setting the right deductible is: Don't make it higher than you have ready available cash. You may find yourself far from home and unable to make repairs.**

Enter Lloyds of London

The above example is for an extended cruise, but still with definite limits. It could apply to a west coast escape artist heading for Alaska,

Hawaii, or deep into Mexico. For an east coast sailor, it could mean Bermuda or the Caribbean. These are the destinations of the majority of voyaging sailors. But for that handful planning on going around the world, or spending four or five years exploring Tahiti, Australia and New Zealand, or working their way to the Mediterranean, there really is only one place they can go to buy insurance: Lloyd's of London.

Another group that may turn to Lloyds are those who don't meet the requirements of American companies, which doesn't necessarily mean they are poor sailors or that their boats are unseaworthy. Even though many American companies won't insure boats under a certain size or over a certain age for anything but local cruising, there are many seamanlike passages being made by competent sailors in well-found boats that just happen to be old or small. If they want insurance, they go to Lloyds of London.

The reason coverage often can be obtained through Lloyds when it cannot in the United States has to do with the unique structure of Lloyds itself. While a yacht policy in the States is underwritten by one large company (i.e. one company assumes the entire risk) a policy with Lloyds means the risk is shared by a number of individual companies. Lloyds of London, actually, is a *building*, not an insurance company. Members of Lloyds (insurance companies or syndicates of companies) meet there to underwrite insurance risks presented by London brokers representing requests from all over the world. A broker might have to spend days or even weeks shopping around the floor of Lloyds, but if he's good the chances are high he can place just about any risk. That's assuming, of course, the insured is willing to pay the rate once the broker has a quote. In some cases the rate has been as high as 20%, but that is an unusually high rate. A more normal figure for a circumnavigation of several years' duration is 4% or 5%.

Some basic differences exist between policies obtained through Lloyds and those written by American companies. With Lloyds, the coverage is "named peril" (you are insured only against specifically named losses), instead of the "all risk" coverage found in most U.S. policies.

I know I will get some arguments here, but the major U.S. companies are pretty good about paying claims quickly. After receiving a surveyor's report and/or estimates on cost of repairs, often they pay off before the work is done. Or, they will pay the yard directly. Payment from Lloyds, however, is slow. It can take as long as four months to get a claim processed. But in fairness to Lloyds, part of the delay is due to communication difficulties. It's one thing to deal with a U.S. company while you are in the U.S. or close by (Canada, perhaps, or the Bahamas) and another matter entirely to file a claim from some obscure port halfway around the world.

Lloyds will not pay until all the work has been completed and paid for by the owner and approved by the surveyor. However, if the claim is extremely large, the insured sometimes can get an advance through his broker.

 **When all else fails, you can usually get insurance through Lloyds of London.**

American policies contain a clause giving the company the right to cancel the insurance, often within ten or 15 days after mailing the notice of cancellation. Check to make sure you'll be able to receive any such notices in time given mail delays at your cruising destinations. Lloyds policies rarely contain such a clause.

Buying Escape Vehicle Insurance

Insurance for cruising boats is highly specialized and complicated. Probably the worst place to purchase it is from a neighborhood insurance company, even a major one, which will tend to view boats as just another piece of property along with cars, houses, works of art and the trailer that carries the boat to and from the launching ramp. The company agent may have a smattering of knowledge about runabouts, ski boats or daysailers, but he is not likely to have the experience or the expertise to make value judgments about a cruising boat and her crew, or to understand the subtleties of a marine surveyor's report. It could cost you extra money. Or, even worse, you could pay good money for inadequate coverage.

An insurance agent who specializes in boats will be more knowledgeable than a general agent. But many such agents represent only one company—although most likely he can obtain a quote from Lloyds by going through a London broker.

For local cruising, contact agents in your area for quotes and sample policies. Decide for yourself which one offers the best coverage at the most reasonable price.

But for extended cruising, your best bet is a reputable, independent broker who specializes in marine insurance. In additon to offering advice on the best type of coverage for your own particular requirements, he can get quotes from four or five American companies as well as from Lloyds of London. Make sure he has a good, established, working relationship with a London broker who knows the ins and outs at Lloyds.

As I've already mentioned, marine insurance is a complicated field, particularly when it comes to handling international claims. Matters involving collisions, sinkings, salvage rights, etc., can become incredibly involved and possibly require the services of an admiralty lawyer. And writing a policy for a yacht heading out for a round the world cruise is not something that happens overnight. Make sure to give yourself enough time ot get the best coverage you can afford.

Much of what has been presented here, especially that relating to Lloyds of London, is based on information supplied by Donald M. Street, Jr. Most cruisers know Donald as owner of the venerable *Iolaire* and author of numerous sailing books, including two volumes of *The Ocean Sailing Yacht* and several volumes of cruising guides for the Caribbean. Don has, in fact, been a broker specializing in marine insurance for the past 20 years. Since any cruiser getting prepared for an offshore voyage who wants to be insured will have questions, I recommend a long talk with a good broker; or you can drop a line to Donald:

Donald M. Street, Jr.
c/o David Payne
Cayser Steel Bowater
38 Dukes Place
London EC3 7LX

Filing an Insurance Claim

As anyone who's ever done it knows, processing an insurance claim can be a time-consuming pain in the neck. While the broker or underwriter should be contacted as soon as possible, steps invariably must be taken to secure the boat or repair damages before specific instructions can be received from the insurance company, particularly if you are in a remote area.

In the United States, the insured may be asked to obtain quotes from several boat yards, or a surveyor may be appointed to direct all repair work.

Either way, keep very careful, accurate records of all money spent. Get receipts for everything purchased. Keep copies of time sheets and make itemized lists of all work performed.

Depending on the area where you are cruising, it may be that you —the insured owner—are the only one capable of making the necessary repairs. While your own "wages" are not normally covered by your insurance policy, exceptions are sometimes made if you can show that you (or a crew member) worked over and above your normal duties and that there was no one locally who could perform the work. Keep a time sheet of hours worked, then give it to the surveyor who generally will place a value on the labor and approve it as a reasonable expense.

When filing a claim, especially from remote areas, delays are inevitable. Do what's necessary to secure and protect your vehicle while awaiting instructions and keep itemized receipts of all expenses.

It also is a good idea to take photos of all damaged areas *before* they are repaired. Keeping accurate records, and presenting them in a logical, legible fashion, will go a long way in speeding up the processing of a claim.

The Option of Self-Insurance

I would never advise anyone *not* to carry insurance on their escape machine. It simply is too personal a decision. But I would suggest to anyone who has made a "no" decision to consider putting some money (a minimum of $2,000) into a separate bank account or a special money market fund, as a type of self-insurance. If the boat is lost, it would be a much-needed cushion to fall back on and to help you get started again.

Another idea, if your long-distance escape is still five years or so away, is to start a self-insurance fund now. Investing as little as $500 a year in a separate fund can grow to a healthy insurance nest egg by the time you're ready to take off.

The other type of self-insurance lies in the soundness of your vehicle and gear and in your own ability and that of your crew. Cruisers who don't carry insurance prefer to put the money into good ground tackle (and plenty of it), and good navigation and safety equipment. They place their highest values on seamanship and sailing ability, and on having a boat that sails well. Wayne Carpenter, who has cruised extensively in the North Atlantic, Caribbean, and along both U.S. coasts, has never carried yacht insurance.

 **If your long-distance escape is still a few years away, consider starting a self-insurance account today. Put $500 a year or more away in a high-yield account. By the time you leave you'll probably have enough money to cover the great majority of possible emergencies.**

"I feel that if my boat washed up on shore, I could salvage enough from it to build another. If it sank in the middle of the ocean, I wouldn't be around to collect, anyway. Cruising is a risk and the umbilical cord has to be snipped somewhere. I prefer to invest the money in ground tackle and safety gear, instead."

 **The best escape vehicle insurance is first-rate equipment and a sound, able crew.**

I cruised for eight years and never carried boat insurance. Our boat now is insured, primarily because it also is financed. As soon as she's paid off we want to go cruising, so we'll have to decide then about insurance but we will keep the insurance through the first year of cruising, at least.

Insurance *is* a personal choice, and one that deserves a great deal of thought. We talked about "risk tolerance" in the investments chapter. Risk tolerance also can apply to insurance. If the boat represents your entire life savings, or if you believe you are too old or would be too distraught at her loss to start over without help—and the worry will keep you awake at night—then insurance is worth any cost just for the peace of mind it brings. Anyone going cruising for the first time, I think, should stay with coasting (there is so much to see along both coasts without crossing an ocean, including going "foreign" to Canada, Mexico and the Bahamas). Keep the boat insured during that time. Allow a year to find out what it's all about, then make a decision about what type of cruising is most appealing, and whether or not to carry insurance.

 **Whether to carry escape vehicle insurance is like choosing an investment strategy. If your decision will keep you awake at night, perhaps you've made the wrong one.**

CHAPTER TEN

Insuring the Body

Prevention always is the best policy

Medical insurance is another one of those financial decisions that has a lot to do with age. Forty seems to be the magic dividing line: People under 40 don't worry about insurance very much, but those folks older than 40 usually think it's a necessity. Certainly with the skyrocketing cost of medical care, many of those who once considered health insurance a waste of money are now giving it some thoughtful attention.

To Buy or Not to Buy

There is no doubt that in cruising as well as most other forms of escape, people are less susceptible to many of the aches and pains and flu bugs that plague shore folks. I know several men who suffered heart attacks, and another with a severe case of ulcers, who took early retirements from their high-pressure jobs and went cruising as much for their health as for anything else. Still, medical emergencies can arise, and an unexpected illness with a prolonged hospital stay can destroy an excape budget for years to come.

My friends George Cranston and Gainor Roberts were cruising the Intracoastal Waterway a few years back. At the time, Gainor was not yet 40 and believed she was in the best of health. One night at anchor near Titusville, Florida, she awoke with severe stomach pains. George rushed her ashore to a hospital emergency room, and the end result was major surgery and almost two weeks in the hospital.

They carry Blue Cross and Blue Shield, at a cost of about $1,000 a year for both of them, which covers 80% of all medical expenses. Without the insurance, they would be working ashore today to pay off the doctor and hospital bills instead of continuing to cruise.

The Moral: Wear Shoes!

Another example of young, healthy people who were glad they had insurance is that of Jack and Pat Tyler, who cruised the eastern seaboard aboard their sloop *Felicity*. The cruise began in the Chesapeake, and almost ended there. While anchored in the Great Wicomico River, a barefooted Jack rowed the dinghy ashore and cut his foot hauling the dinghy up the beach. It was a small cut, and he didn't pay much attention to it other than to clean it when he got back to *Felicity*.

But the back waters of the Chesapeake experience little change of tide, and strange forms of bacteria and, sadly, pollution lurk in the muddy bottom. By the time Jack got to Annapolis an infection was attacking the bone in his foot. Surgery was performed, followed by extensive therapy—for a total of 31 days in the hospital. Interestingly, Jack and Pat had decided to drop their insurance when they quit their jobs.

"We figured we didn't need it, we were both so healthy." They changed their minds at the last minute, switching from a group policy to a private Blue Cross/Blue Shield major medical plan at a cost of $100 a month. Obviously they are glad they made that decision. But Jack says the real moral to this story is simple: "Wear shoes!"

All the offshore cruising people I talked to who do carry insurance carry only major medical and hospitalization, not a standard health policy that covers routine visits to a doctor or clinic, or normal medications or prescriptions. Their policies generally have a hefty deductible ($1,000–$2,000) to reduce the cost, and they try to keep that amount set aside for emergencies. Table 1 gives an example of typical insurance plans available for major medical coverage.

Insurance companies take any number of factors into account when figuring the cost of a policy—age, present state of health and where you lived when you got the policy. But, unlike boat insurance, they don't consider the areas where you may be traveling. Some companies even consider a person's sex—giving different rates to men and women of the same age and general health. If someone has an existing condition, few companies will cover that condition, even for a higher premium. For example, when I was in my twenties I had cornea transplant surgery in both eyes. While I am in good health and it is easy for me to obtain insurance, I have yet to find a company that will insure me for anything at all going wrong with my eyes.

TABLE 1 MAJOR MEDICAL INSURANCE COVERAGE

Chart courtesy of Blue Cross of California.

	Major Protection			Basic Protection	
				Hospitalization	Major Medical
DEDUCTIBLE (Maximum of 2 per family.)	$200	$500	$1,000	None	$200
BLUE CROSS PAYS 80% UNTIL BLUE CROSS PAYMTS. REACH:	$6,000	$8,000	$8,000	365 days, renewable after 28 days, 50% for Mental Disorders.	$500,000
NO LOSS-MAXIMUM: BLUE CROSS PAYS 100% FOR BALANCE OF YEAR UP TO:	$2 million	$2 million	$2 million	None	None
	The following benefits listed are identical for "200," "500," "1000" Plans. Benefits are provided after the deductible is satisfied.			The following benefits listed combine hospitalization and Major Medical. Benefits for hospitalization start at once. Those for Major Medical are provided after the deductible is satisfied.	
Hospital Services	80% of charges.			80% of charges.	
Skilled Nursing Facility	80% of charges.			80% of charges.	
Maternity (Subscriber and Spouse only)	80% of charges to maximum $1000 benefit payment for normal delivery and elective abortions. Cesarean section and other complications of pregnancy payable as any other illness.			Not covered.	
Mental Disorders/ Alcohol Detoxification/	50% of charges up to 30 day maximum per calendar year.			50% of charges up to 30 days maximum per calendar year.	

Surgeon, Assistant Surgeon, Anesthetist	80% of UCR*	80% of UCR* after Major Medical deductible satisfied.
Outpatient Emergency Hospital Care	80% of UCR*	100% hospital's charge for minor surgery and for accident care within 72 hours of the accidental injury.
Outpatient X-Ray and Laboratory Examination	80% of UCR*	80% of charges for pre-admission testing within 7 days of members's admission for inpatient or outpatient surgery.
Radiation Therapy	80% of UCR*	80% of UCR,* after deductible is satisfied.
Physical Therapy	80% of UCR*	Covered under Home Health Care.
Mental Disorders (Outpatient)	Up to $25 per visit to a maximum of 50 visits per calendar year.	Not covered.
Doctors Visits in Hospital, Office or Home	80% of UCR*	80% of UCR* in Hospital only, after deductible satisfied.
Home Health Care (when approved by a licensed agency)	80% of UCR* to a maximum of 60 visits per calendar year.	80% of UCR* to a maximum of 60 visits per calendar year after deductible satisfied.
Ambulance (surface)	80% of UCR*	Up to $50 to a hospital for eligible in-patient admission only.
Prosthetic Appliances	80% of UCR*	Not covered.
Prescription Drugs	80% of UCR*	Not covered.
Waiting Periods, pre-existing Conditions	6 months	6 months
Lifetime Maximums	$2,000,000 maximum benefit payment.	$500,000 maximum benefit payment
Family Deductibles	2 per Family per calendar year.	2 per Family per calendar year.

*UCR = Usual, Customary and Reasonable Charges as determined by Blue Cross of California.

This is a summary of available options only. It is not a contract. All Benefits referenced are subject to any applicable Exclusions and/or Limitations in your Agreement and are contingent upon member eligibility at the time services are rendered.

One way to keep down the cost of medical insurance during your escape is to carry a high deductible. Try to keep that amount set aside somewhere in case of an emergency.

As a very general rule of thumb, figure $1,000 to $1,500 a year for major medical and hospitalization insurance with a $1,000 deductible for a couple in good health in their mid-forties. Sometimes, instead of a deductible, a policy will cover a percentage—usually 80%. Someone older will probably pay more.

For an idea of what one company charges—and the rates *are* pretty typical—take a look at Table 2. It gives the cost of the plans described in Table 1. You can see the difference in cost based on age. These rates are for one particular geographical area (three counties in Southern California).

Rates for group insurance are always lower than an individual policy. It's a good idea for anyone who works for a company that provides health benefits at a group rate to investigate possibly continuing the insurance before quitting their job. It may be possible that, by paying the premiums themselves, they can continue coverage, at least for awhile.

Rather than quitting, it may be advantageous to take a leave of absence, since this maintains employment status and allows group coverage rates to remain in force. I know one couple who were able to do this for a full year. The husband took a leave of absence in the first place because he planned on returning to his old job. He discovered he could keep the insurance coverage if he paid the premiums. Just for the record, at the end of the year he officially quit and they kept cruising, with occasional three or four-month work stops at shore jobs to replenish the cruising fund.

Most major health policies will provide worldwide coverage. But make very sure of this before casting off dock lines. Aetna, for instance, won't cover anyone outside the United States. Be sure the

TABLE 2 **MONTHLY COSTS OF THE INSURANCE PLANS SHOWN IN TABLE 1**

Chart courtesy of Blue Cross of California.

MONTHLY COSTS (AREA 4)

	Major Protection			Basic Protection
	$200 Deductible	$500 Deductible	$1,000 Deductible	$200 Deductible
Youngest adult under 30 years old				
Single	$ 56.25	$ 42.19	$ 32.06	$ 34.88
Two Party (2 adults)	$110.25	$ 82.13	$ 61.88	$ 67.50
Family (adults & children)	$157.27	$113.34	$ 84.69	$ 94.50
Adult & Child	$103.27	$ 73.41	$ 52.88	$ 61.88
Adult & Children	$126.79	$ 88.99	$ 63.28	$ 75.38
Youngest adult 30-39 years old				
Single	$ 81.00	$ 58.50	$ 47.25	$ 48.94
Two Party (2 adults)	$159.75	$114.75	$ 92.25	$ 95.63
Family (adults & children)	$206.77	$145.97	$113.06	$122.63
Adult & Child	$128.02	$ 89.72	$ 68.06	$ 75.94
Adult & Children	$151.54	$105.30	$ 78.47	$ 89.44
Youngest adult 40-90 years old				
Single	$108.00	$ 74.25	$ 59.06	$ 64.69
Two Party (2 adults)	$213.75	$146.25	$115.88	$127.13
Family (adults & children)	$260.77	$177.47	$136.69	$154.13
Adult & Child	$155.02	$105.47	$ 79.88	$ 91.69
Adult & Children	$178.54	$1121.05	$ 90.28	$105.19
Youngest adult 50-59 years old				
Single	$139.50	$ 98.44	$ 78.75	$ 87.75
Two Party (2 adults)	$276.75	$194.63	$155.25	$173.25
Family (adults & children)	$323.77	$225.84	$176.06	$200.25
Adult & Child	$186.52	$129.66	$ 99.56	$114.75
Adult & Children	$210.04	$145.24	$109.97	$128.25
Youngest adult 60-64 years old				
Single	$155.25	$110.81	$ 87.75	$101.25
Two Party (2 adults)	$308.25	$219.38	$173.25	$200.25
Family (adults & children)	$355.27	$250.59	$194.06	$227.25
Adult & Child	$202.27	$142.03	$108.56	$128.25
Adult & Children	$225.79	$157.61	$118.97	$141.75

AREA 4 COUNTIES: Orange, Santa Barbara, Ventura.

policy is without geographical limitations. And being insured doesn't mean that any hospital anywhere in the world is going to fill out all those forms, then sit back and wait for an insurance company in a foreign country to ante up. It's more likely they'll want to be paid— right then and there—and let *you* worry about getting reimbursed from the insurance company.

While most cruisers I talked with carry Blue Cross/Blue Shield, there are, of course, many other companies (Prudential, Kaiser, etc.). You can shop around or contact a broker who deals with several companies, explain your travel plans and discuss the kind of insurance you are looking for, and let the broker make recommendations.

One world cruiser, who has opted for no health insurance, said she and her husband have a special fund of several thousand dollars set aside for medical emergencies. It is a separate account, not part of their regular checking account. She believes it is enough to cover a "real" emergency—one that would require immediate admittance to a hospital or clinic emergency room. But for a serious illness, or a problem requiring eventual surgery, she feels better knowing there is enough money in the fund to allow her to fly back to the States to her own family doctor, rather than relying on possibly questionable care in whatever obscure port they happen to be moored. The only problem with this is that if extensive medical care is required, there is still no insurance to cover the costs.

"Somewhere," she said, "you have to draw the line, or you'll never go cruising." She is in good health, capable of earning a living, and young enough to rebound from any setback.

 **Make sure your health insurance policy covers you wherever your escape leads you. And figure out how much cash you'll need to pay for health care abroad while waiting for your insurance company to reimburse you.**

How About Trying Self-Insurance?

To a lot of people "self-insured" really means no insurance at all. But it shouldn't. Like the world cruiser mentioned earlier, a specified amount can be set aside to cover medical emergencies. It's best that this money be kept separate from a regular checking or savings account. Otherwise it is just too tempting to spend it on something else, probably something much more fun. Of course, it doesn't have to be in a bank. It can be a separate fund invested in a money market, mutual fund, government bonds, any type of investment that can be tapped reasonably fast.

As a minimum, I would try to keep $2,000 in the medical fund. Even if you carry insurance, it's a good idea to have this fund to cover the cost of the policy's deductible, or to use as up-front money when a hospital insists on immediate payment and you must work out your own reimbursement.

Some money should be earmarked for travel, particularly if your escape takes you to remote islands or sparsely-populated areas. Small harbor towns in third-world countries are not going to have the extensive medical facilities we take for granted in the States. For a major problem, you are likely to have to travel—by plane, train, or donkey cart—to a major city where better medical care is available.

Another Kind of Insurance

I like to think of self-insured as meaning more than just setting money aside. I think of it as self-preparedness, or self-help; and in many ways I believe being able to take care of yourself is more important than an insurance policy. When you're hundreds of miles offshore or on the top of a remote mountain and someone cracks a rib or develops a high fever and severe pain, no insurance policy and no amount of money is going to help. It can help when you reach civilization, but it's more important to make sure that the sick or injured person *gets* to civilization to begin with.

Certainly every adult should have at least a rudimentary knowledge of first aid, and every escape vehicle should be equipped with a complete first aid kit. That's adequate for day-sailing and weekending, but anyone heading off for an extended voyage owes it to themselves and their shipmates to be better prepared. Even coastal cruisers can, because of bad weather or equipment failure, experience long delays in getting outside assistance or getting ashore for emergency care. The following is a rundown on organizations that can offer assistance to cruising sailors and other travelers in a medical emergency.

U.S. COAST GUARD

When coastal cruising in the United States, most sailors in an emergency think first of calling the Coast Guard. The Coast Guard is, indeed, equipped to handle medical emergencies. It can be reached on VHF channel 16. In some areas the Coast Guard also monitors channel 9 on CB radio, but this is a local option and cannot always be relied upon.

Whenever the Coast Guard receives a medical emergency call, it automatically assumes the possibility of transfer at sea (either by boat or helicopter) and alerts all personnel who would be involved in a rescue effort. It does this in the belief that it's better to be ready and then call the rescue off, than to cause needless delays in the event a transfer *is* required. Despite the occasional horror stories that circulate about the Coast Guard, the personnel I spoke with all appeared both knowledgeable and genuinely concerned about handling medical emergencies. I found it reassuring to learn the effort the Coast Guard would expend to help someone in trouble.

While the average Coast Guardsman will not and cannot dispense medical advice, the service does maintain a list of medical people on call at any time, ranging from flight surgeons to medical officers to civilian physicians at local hospitals. As with any branch of the government, the Coast Guard follows certain procedures. If you should ever have need to call them, be prepared to relate the following information about the stricken crewmember:

- The symptoms and overall condition of the patient.
- When the symptoms started.
- Temperature.
- Pulse.
- Mobility (can he/she walk?).
- Location of any pain or swelling.
- If the patient is experiencing vomiting or diarrhea.

- Any medications that have been administered and what supplies are aboard.

Considering the inherent risks in transferring people at sea, especially by helicopter, it's better to treat someone aboard if possible, make them comfortable, and get to shoreside facilities as quickly as you can.

 **The best insurance doesn't cost anything at all—except the time and energy it takes to be self-sufficient and prepared for medical emergencies. Insurance policies don't stop calamities from happening. With or without insurance, prevention *is* the best policy.**

MEDICAL ADVISORY SYSTEMS HOTLINE (MASH)

Originally designed as a service for the merchant marine, MASH was recently made available to pleasure boat owners as well. the subscription service costs $45 a year and provides unlimited access to medical advice by direct contact with a team of physicians at the MASH medical response center in Owings, Maryland. A team is on duty year-round, 24 hours a day. One subscription to MASH provides coverage for two subscribers, their children and any guests on board. Subscribers fill out medical history forms that are entered into a computer for immediate access by the medical team. Additionally, MASH provides an Emergency Medical Protocol Manual and First Aid Guide to aid subscribers in communicating with the doctors and to help them follow recommended procedures.

A communications specialist at the center receives the calls and figures out the best way to maintain contact with the subscriber, not always an easy task considering the vagaries of marine radio and the limitations of many power systems on small boats. Contact can be established in several ways:

- VHF RADIO: Call the marine operator and give MASH's national 800 toll-free number.
- SSB RADIO: MASH is licensed to use 19 channels on SSB. Crystal frequencies are given on the MASH identification card.
- Ham radio operators can patch through to the Maryland number at the medical response center.
- The U.S. Coast Guard has agreed to help subscribers in reaching the medical response center.
- If you are ashore in a foreign country, call the international operator and give the Maryland number in the United States (not the toll free number).

MASH could be of great value to coastal cruisers equipped with a VHF radio, and to offshore voyagers carrying more sophisticated equipment—single sideband (SSB) or a ham radio. Since one of the basic purposes of amateur (ham) radio operation is to render emergency assistance, a ham operator could put you in contact with a doctor or a hospital. The advantage of being a MASH subscriber, however, is that the doctors at the center have access to your medical history, something that could be critically important. A ham operator wouldn't necessarily be able to reach your own personal physician back in the States, who might be on the golf course or on vacation.

Without SSB radio or ham equipment and a license to operate it, I don't think the MASH service would be nearly as helpful to long-distance cruisers as to those cruising locally. If you must wait until you reach shore—any shore—to get medical assistance, you are more likely to seek help locally than to make an international phone call. Hands-on care by a competent physician is bound to be better than even the best advice given via telephone.

For complete information about subscribing to MASH, call the toll-free number 1-800-368-2268. In Maryland, call 301-855-5556; or write to:

Medical Advisory Systems, Inc.
Pleasure Craft Division
Box 193 Chaneyville Junction
Owings, MD 20736

IAMAT

The International Association for Medical Assistance to Travelers (IAMAT) was founded in 1960 to provide a source of competent medical help for people traveling outside their own country. Joining IAMAT is an excellent idea for anyone who plans on escaping outside the United States. There is no charge for membership although, since its only support comes from voluntary contributions, IAMAT does appreciate a donation (which is tax deductible). Membership provides the following:

- MEMBERSHIP CARD: Identifies the holder as a member entitled to IAMAT services at fixed rates.
- WORLD DIRECTORY: Lists physicians in 125 countries and territories who speak either English or another language (usually French) in addition to their native language, although most do speak English; who have had medical training in North America or Europe and have passed an IAMAT review of their qualificaitons; and who have agreed to the fee schedule set by IAMAT. The fees are $20 for an office visit, $25 for a house call, and $30 for a visit at night or on Sundays or local holidays. The fees, of course, don't include lab work like x-rays and blood tests.
- TRAVELER'S CLINICAL RECORD: A small booklet to be filled out by the member's own physician. It provides medical history and an immunization record that can be referred to by any IAMAT physician.
- WORLD IMMUNIZATION CHART: Lists immunization recommendations for 200 countries and territories, as well as giving information about preventive measures.
- WORLD MALARIA RISK CHART AND PROTECTION GUIDE.
- WORLD SCHISTOSOMIASIS RISK CHART AND INFORMATION GUIDE. Schistosomiasis is a tropical disease that can be contracted by swimming or wading in fresh water.

It only takes a small effort to join IAMAT, but the information you receive on becoming a member can prove invaluable. It's fun to communicate with gestures and smiles at the native marketplace, but trying to explain precisely what hurts to a doctor—who speaks a different language—is another story entirely. With IAMAT's directory, the chances of finding a qualified English-speaking physician are greatly enhanced. To join IAMAT, write to:

IAMAT
736 Center Street
Lewiston, NY 14092

Emergency Medical Training

It's fine to have insurance and/or money in the bank, and it's good to have a boat or camper equipped with radio(s) that can summon help or seek advice from far away. All this will contribute to a feeling of security. But, in reality, it's a false sense of security. For a boat in the middle of the ocean or an RV in the middle of a wilderness, help can be a long time in coming and precious minutes or even hours can be wasted in trying to make radio connections. The only security that is "real" is the knowledge that you are prepared to handle a medical emergency *yourself.*

A first aid course and a course in CPR (cardio-pulmonary resuscitation) is probably enough training for coastal cruisers who can reach professional help ashore within a short period of time or, for that matter, who can be assisted relatively easily by Coast Guard personnel.

Most cruisers find a session with their own personal physician helpful, provided he or she really understands what it means to be at sea in a small boat. At least he can write prescriptions for medications not available over the counter. Another option is a yacht club fleet surgeon, who presumably is a sailor, and most likely one with at least some offshore experience.

Sitting in on an EMT (emergency medical technician) course at a local college or rescue squad is helpful to some, but both the medical terminology and the course content is often too difficult for the average layman with no previous medical training. And such courses naturally assume that hospitals and doctors are close at hand. A yacht at sea is not going to have the equipment found in a hospital emergency room or in a mobile intensive care unit.

There is, however, a course designed specifically for the offshore sailor, the Intensive Survey of Medical Emergency Care, conceived and directed by Dr. Robert Kingston, an emergency room physician *and* a sailor. Dr. Kingston believes all emergencies can be dealt with in a competent manner by an intelligent, prepared adult. His course is anything but another rehearsed first aid course. He points out that if someone suffers a heart attack, it's important to know CPR, but knowing what to do afterwards is equally important.

Far off the beaten track, the only real medical insurance is being able to handle the emergency yourself.

As the name implies, the course is intensive: 26 hours compressed into one evening and two days. It is not just lectures. A "hands-on" approach is used, with carefully supervised skill sessions that teach, among other things, how to take and interpret vital signs (temperature, blood pressure, etc.), how to stop hemorrhage, how to make splints, how to give injections and how to maintain an airway.

A workbook, written and constantly updated by Dr. Kingston, is provided with the course. The workbook becomes an excellent on-board reference text, with diagnosis and treatment explained in a way that can be quickly understood and implemented. He stresses that the course is neither written nor taught in "medicalese," but is presented in terminology that the average adult can understand.

"This is not to say the course talks down to the layman," says Kingston, "Rather, it challenges him to strive for the highest quantity and quality of learning of which he is capable."

Additionally, Kingston has compiled a list of drugs and supplies that can be carried on a small boat, and the course provides instruction in their use.

Lessons covered in the three-day session include:

- VITAL SIGNS—what they are and how to take them.
- SHOCK, INCLUDING ALLERGIC SHOCK
- BLOOD VESSEL DISEASES
- CHEST PAIN—how to distinguish different types, and how to deal with it
- CHEST INJURIES—from the inconvenient to the life threatening
- BASIC LIFE-SAVING

- EMERGENCIES OF EXTREME HEAT AND COLD
- DIVING INJURIES AND NEAR DROWNING
- SKIN INJURIES AND DISEASES OF THE SKIN
- INTRAMUSCULAR AND SUBCUTANEOUS INJECTIONS
- BELLY PAIN—sizing up the situation
- URINARY INFECTIONS AND KIDNEY STONES
- BACK INJURIES
- BONE BREAKS AND JOINT INJURIES
- SEIZURES, STROKES AND MENINGITIS
- AIRWAY PROBLEMS—how to distinguish the trivial and treat the life-threatening
- EYE EMERGENCIES, INCLUDING A SKILL SESSION IN HOW TO EX- AMINE AN EYE
- DRUGS YOU NEED TO KNOW—benefits vs. hazards
- POISONINGS
- VENOMOUS AND POISONOUS MARINE LIFE

Tuition for the course is $275 for one person or $495 for two people registering together. Don't balk at the price, it is worth every penny and then some. Up until this year, the course was only offered in California—several sessions in the San Francisco area and several in Southern California (Newport Beach and Laguna Beach). Kingston is now offering the course in Boston, Massachusetts, and Fort Lauderdale, Florida. For information on upcoming sessions, write:

> Intensive Survey of Medical Emergency Care
> 25381-G Alicia Parkway, Suite 104
> Laguna Hills, California 92653

or call Dr. Kingston at (714) 831-3084.

The course provides something else I believe is equally as important as knowledge. Shearlean Duke, a cruising sailor who is as timid as I am in certain respects, sums it up pretty well. She says, "While the information and skills we learned from Dr. Kingston's course are of great value, in retrospect, the real benefits of the course for us may not lie in its content so much as in the context in which it is presented. Kingston is so sincere that it rubs off on you in such a way that feeling silly or embarrassed about playing doctor will never keep you from doing the right thing."

CHAPTER ELEVEN

Escaping on Land:

By Highway and Byway

Most of the information contained in this book applies to any means of escape be it by boat, RV, bicycle, or backpack. Getting medical help, taking care of bills and business back home or re-entering the job market are of concern to every successful escape artist. Most of the insurance chapter, however, deals with boats since boat insurance, particularly if you are sailing thousands of miles from home port, is complicated and expensive. But to insure an RV, all you need to prove your competence is a valid driver's license. No one is going to question your ability to read a road map or ask for resumes detailing you and your "crew's" past camping experience. Just as there are items that apply only to a sailing escape, considerations exist of interest only to those planning to cruise by land.

Car or RV?

Some people make escapes in cars, but we're not really talking about "vacations" here—spending a month at a resort or a few weeks touring the southwest. To me, and to most RVers I've talked with, "escaping" has much to do with being self-sufficient and self-contained, taking our homes along with us. It doesn't surprise me in the least that many RV folks refer to their traveling homes as "land yachts."

Certainly a car or a station wagon is easier to drive and gets better mileage than a motor home or a car towing a trailer. But with some practice, it doesn't take long to get the hang of driving a big rig: to learn the gears, the tricks of backing up, parking and maneuvering in tight spots, and learning where you can and cannot go. When I first got my camper, I drove into one of those multi-storied parking garages. The low-overhead sign didn't register in my mind until I heard an awful crunch—my roof-mounted propane tank was dangling by its hose, banging into the rear window. I won't make that mistake again!

The American Automobile Association (AAA), in its booklet "Your Driving Costs," suggests two people traveling by car should plan on

154

spending around $50 a day for meals (add another $10 a day for each child if it's a family trip), $51 a day for lodging, and $7 for every 100 miles for gas and oil (assuming an average of 22 miles a gallon). Multiplying just the food and lodging, it comes out to over $3,000 for just one month!

By comparison, campgrounds in state and national parks average about $6 a night, private RV parks about $8–$12 a night. Prices will vary, depending on whether you are fully self-contained or want hook-ups for electricity, water and sewage. People over 62, by the way, can get a "Golden Age Passport" at any national park that gives them a 50% discount at all national parks.

As for food, I don't think there is anyone who doesn't know the difference between eating a meal out and buying groceries to cook for themselves.

 **Escaping by land doesn't have to be any more expensive than you want it to be. Try cooking your own food. Avoid expensive motels. And don't use your fuel-guzzling vehicle for sightseeing—take along bicycles or motor scooters, instead.**

One alternative for hardy outdoor lovers is to travel by car and tow along a tent trailer. Often the "car" in this case is a van, a station wagon, or something with four-wheel drive.

It's true that the cost per mile to drive a big rig is much higher than driving an automobile. George VonSchlatter, who has traveled by RV throughout the United States, Canada and Mexico, told me his 35-foot motor home averages 7 miles a gallon. But he's quick to point out that he only drives "from one ponit to the next." He doesn't use the rig for sightseeing. Instead, he carries two motor bikes. He and his wife Carol will drive to a particular spot where they want to spend several days or several weeks, park the motor home, and use the bikes for local travel. They also carry a 13-foot inflatable boat and an outboard engine. Many people with large rigs will tow a compact car along with them. Over the long haul, this approach can mean a tremendous reduction in the *total* cost-per-mile of driving.

There are other, less tangible reasons for escaping by a motor home instead of by car. Ask anyone who does a lot of business traveling by car—after a while, restaurant food all tastes the same. It's fun to eat out occasionally, to sample local or ethnic foods, to try something new and different. But eating out three meals a day, day in and day out, whether it's at a roadside cafe or the fanciest restaurant in town, just gets *old*. It's so much better to have your own food with you, and be able to choose where you want to dine. This is even more critical if you are traveling with small children. They'll be much happier companions if their diet remains the same familiar food they were used to "back home."

Depending on the size of your rig, it can be a treat to rent a room occasionally. I have a Volkswagon camper/van that's completely self-contained. It's about as small as you can get but it has a double bunk, two-burner stove, sink and water tank, an amazing (to me) amount of storage space, a camper potty and a solar SunShower. You bet it's great to stop at a motel occasionally and stand in the shower for as long as I feel like under all that hot running water. But most of the time I'm much happier snuggling down at night under my own familiar cozy quilt, knowing there's no checkout time and hearing only the sound of wind in the pine trees or surf on the beach, instead of the roar of traffic along Highway 101.

Size deserves consideration, too. Taz and I find the miniscule accommodations of the van perfectly comfortable. With the sun roof raised, we can even stand up. But remember that we both have been living on boats for years. We are used to small spaces, and we love to get away by land for a few days or a few weeks. But for a real escape, a many-months trip across the United States perhaps, we would opt for something larger. Anyone moving from a house or a large apartment is likely to develop "cabin fever" if they choose too small a rig. Just like moving onto a boat, if it's going to be your home, you want room for some of your personal treasures, a bed that doesn't have to be converted every night from a settee, and room to stretch your legs and relax after a long day on the road.

Before you decide what size vehicle you need for your escape, carefully consider your space needs. Anyone moving from a large house or apartment into a mini van is likely to get a bad case of cabin fever.

Trip Planning

While there may be one or two cruising guides for a particular area available to sailors, the amount of literature available for land travel is nothing short of mind-boggling. One trip to a newsstand will reveal a myriad of magazines devoted to motor homes, trailering, camping and hiking. Bookstore shelves are lined with volumes devoted to land travel in just about every corner of the world.

A good reference to take along is one of the Rand McNally guides to campgrounds and trailer parks. There are several editions for various sections of the United States as well as Canada and Mexico. Each book contains pertinent data about private parks in addition to state and national sites. Since they're from Rand McNally they naturally contain detailed maps.

Write ahead to cities and towns you'll be visiting. The local Chamber of Commerce is always a good place to start, and most major cities have Visitors and Convention Bureaus. They usually send back street maps and stacks of brochures on points of interest, excursions, shops and restaurants, suggestions of all kinds about places to go and things to do.

You can join numerous clubs and associations. They are not expensive and offer newsletters and magazines, guides to campsites, discounts at various RV parks, and for those who like to travel as part of a group—organized caravans and rallies. Some of the larger national clubs are:

- The Family Motor Coach Association
  8291 Clough Pike
  Cincinnati, OH 45244

- The National Campers and Hikers Association
  7172 Transit Road
  Buffalo, NY 14221
- North American Family Campers Association
  Box 308
  Newburyport, MA 01950

Auto Clubs, such as AAA, also are a wealth of information. However, at least in the case of AAA, you "join" by buying car insurance and they only supply their literature to members.

Another place to go for information is trailer supply or RV stores; not just your own local one but stores in areas you are visiting. Many of them have courtesy desks that supply local maps, listings of nearby campsites and parks, and frequently discount coupons as well.

Not everyone wants to stop at a campsite every night. Parking in an "unauthorized" space can be tricky, however. Pick the spot with care or you could find yourself being rudely awakened in the middle of the night by local police telling you to move on, or writing you a ticket. Many rest areas along national highways allow overnight parking. Sometimes you can pull into a gas station, fill up the tank, and a friendly attendant will allow you to park overnight—far from scenic, but it's free. I have on two occasions parked in the middle of a deserted shopping mall parking lot without being hassled, but undoubtedly I was just lucky. And sadly, more and more beaches in the U.S. are becoming littered with no-no signs: "No overnight parking, no camping, no RVs, no this, no that . . ."

Sometimes you can stay for free (sometimes you can stay forever) on unfenced Bureau of Land Management (BLM) land, as long as health regulations are complied with. Whole communities have sprung up on BLM land in Alaska, and I have heard of other ones in Arizona. I'm sure there are many others.

Local knowledge can often help—talk to other RVers, campers, truckers, and as I mentioned earlier, local RV stores.

Readying the Rig

To get to where you're going, you must depend on your engine. The more you know about its care, the better. By all means carry an owner's manual and/or a repair manual for the engine, as well as for any other equipment such as portable generators, air conditioners, refrigeration systems, etc.

If you don't feel confident doing a pre-trip tuneup yourself, take the vehicle to a good mechanic. But explain what you're doing and watch over his shoulder while he's working. Don't be afraid to ask questions. Even if it costs more because your presence makes the job take longer, it's money well spent.

Some routine maintenance checks that every long-distance driver should be able to perform include:

- Check all fluid levels (oil, transmission fluid, brake fluid, windshield wiper fluid)
- Check the fan belt and generator belt
- Check the battery level and battery connections
- Check the radiator and cooling system
- Check all radiator, water pump and fuel hoses
- Check the air filter
- Check all lights to be sure they operate—headlights, brake lights, turn indicators, etc.
- Check the condition of the windshield wiper blades
- Check tire condition, lugnuts, and tire pressure
- Check outside vents, such as those for stove, refrigerator, air conditioner, etc.
- Check propane tanks and all connections.

I am a firm believer in carrying a good tool kit and as many spare parts as possible. Even if you are sticking to the main roads in the U.S., an auto parts store or gas station in a small town may not carry every size of even a simple item such as a fan belt. As a minimum, take along a few extra cans of oil, transmission and brake fluid, distilled water for the batteries, extra belts, and a spare set of windshield wiper blades.

Another "spare part" to remember is an extra set of keys. Buy one of the little magnetic key boxes and hide it somewhere outside, such as under the hood or in a wheel well.

If your escape includes a winter holiday, a ski trip perhaps, or going anywhere where the temperature will drop below freezing, make sure the RV's interior heating system is sufficient. Check the seals around windows and doors and find out what kind of insulation has been built in, if any. You may want to add more. Definitely add insulation around water tanks and pipes and hoses. Make sure the propane tanks are filled with propane and not butane. Propane will work at temperatures well below freezing but butane will not.

Provisioning may or may not be as complicated as what we discuss in Chapter Three, "Budgeting Your Resources." It depends on where you're going. Anyone heading deep into Mexico or South America will plan as carefully as someone heading out to sea. Generally, it's true on land that if there's a road there will be a town and a store somewhere down the line. But small towns in remote areas may not carry your favorite brand or even the particular item you want. And it's just an awfully nice feeling to know you can stay in some beautiful corner of a wilderness paradise for weeks or even months if that's what you feel like doing, without having to look for a grocery store every few days.

 If your escape will take you anyplace cold, make sure to check whether your vehicle is adequately insulated. And be sure your stove/heater tanks have been filled with propane, not butane, which won't flow below freezing.

Radios

While boats generally have VHF radio, single sideband, or a ham rig, RVs are usually equipped with Citizens Band (CB) or sometimes a ham set (see Chapter Eight, "Getting News From Afar"). No operator license is required for CB, only a station license. Call signs are assigned by the FCC when the station license is issued.

CB has 40 channels, between the frequencies of 26.965 and 27.405 MHz. Channel 9 has been designated for emergency use and "traveler assistance."

CB is simple to use and easy enough to learn. However, the FCC requires that all stations carry a current copy of the CB Rules and

Regulations, Subpart D of Part 95, Personal Radio Services. A new, updated edition is issued each year. Order one from:

Superintendent of Documents
Government Printing Office
Washington, D.C. 20402

Permanent Addresses

While this topic was covered in detail in Chapter Eight, there are a few points that may be of interest to anyone escaping by land.

Depending on the state you live in, it may be advantageous to use the mail-forwarding service as your permanent address. For example, TRA (Texas Residents Association), a forwarding service in Arlington, Texas, is used by many travelers because Texas has no state income tax and no property tax on vehicles registered in Texas. The cost of auto registration is low. Some examples:

- Car, up to 3,500 pounds—$15.80
- Truck, 4800 pounds—$21.42
- Travel Trailer, 7,400 pounds—$32.86

TRA points out that their address alone will not qualify you as a resident. You must spend some time there and show that you intend to be a resident by maintaining some ties, such as a permanent address (TRA), a bank account or a driver's license. TRA will mail to members the Texas Driving Handbook and a list of banks. The tax savings could make it worthwhile to include Texas in your itinerary. Similarly, Nevada offers definite benefits for anyone spending a long period of time on the road. Escape artists using the Traveler's Overnight Mail Association (TOMA) mail-forwarding services (see address page 107) can save on income and property tax, on some registration fees and can use their mail drop as a home for insurance purposes.

CHAPTER TWELVE

Managing the Final Escape

Where there's a will there's a way

Part of the art of managing your escape is leaving home with your eyes wide open, fully prepared for whatever your adventure may bring. It may mean finding the perfect palm tree-lined Polynesian cove in which to spend your remaining days. But it also means settling your affairs in the event your escape becomes the kind from which there is no return. Plainly speaking, it's silly to leave home without a will.

Laws on writing wills vary from state to state. This chapter, then, will address general issues more than specific ones; although there are some points to consider no matter what state you claim as your residence.

 **Plainly speaking, you're a fool if you leave home without a will—unless you trust the government to settle your estate fairly.**

Do You Need a Will?

The answer is yes. Even though more than half the people in the United States die without a will (it's called dying "intestate"), it still is very important that every adult have a valid will. Without a will, each state's intestacy laws will apply and the disposition of property (both real and personal) may be a far cry from what you probably want.

There are certain types of property that can be exempt from intestacy laws. One type is the proceeds from life insurance policies and retirement plans, assuming you named a beneficiary. Another is property, like a boat or camper, that is owned by more than one person, depending on the wording of the ownership agreement. If two or more people own the boat as "joint tenants with right of survivorship," and

164

one owner dies, then his or her share automatically transfers to the surviving owners. Intestacy laws do not apply.

If the boat (or any other piece of property) is owned jointly by a husband and wife with no other owners, it can be owned as "tenants by the entirety." If the documents are written this way and one spouse dies the boat will automatically go to the surviving one, again avoiding any intestacy laws. However, if the boat is owned by "tenants in common," and one owner dies without a will, then intestacy laws will apply and the surviving owner could find himself with a new, and not necessarily welcome, co-owner.

In states with community property laws, full ownership of community property purchased in one name only will not automatically go to the surviving spouse. Only half will belong to him or her, and the other half will be subject to intestacy laws—unless there is a will. "Community" property is anything purchased by either spouse after the marriage. "Separate" property refers to anything owned by either spouse before the marriage, and it remains as separate property after marriage.

Two friends of mine, who have been cruising in the Caribbean for several years, have been living together aboard for more than ten years. For reasons of their own they have chosen to remain unmarried. Jim is sole owner of the boat. Realizing that if he died, Karen would be left virtually homeless since intestacy laws would not recognize her as a family member (she could go to court claiming common-law marriage, but at great expense), he had a will drawn up specifically naming her as beneficiary of the boat.

Who Should Write the Will

The best person to write a will is an attorney specializing in wills, trusts and estates. He or she will be intimately familiar with your state's laws and can give advice on wording and clauses that can save tax dollars for your beneficiaries and ensure they won't have to go through tedious probate proceedings to validate the will.

People with small estates can, and do, write their own wills. Books are available at most libraries that explain how it's done. And with an estate whose total value is under $50,000, there is little concern about either federal or state taxes. However, statutory rules must be strictly adhered to or the validity of a will can be questioned in court. One tiny mistake can cause the will to be declared invalid. If you do decide to write your own will, at least have it checked over by an attorney before you consider it complete. Some points to keep in mind are:

- The will must be in writing and signed by the testator (the person making the will) before witnesses. "In writing" generally means *typed,* although occasionally "holographic" wills (written entirely in the individual's own handwriting) and "noncuptive" wills (oral wills) are deemed valid. But this is generally something a court must decide.
- A will should be typed, using the same typewriter throughout, with no erasures and no written corrections of names or figures.
- A will can be revoked wholly or in part by "operation of law," such as the death of a spouse, birth of another child, etc.; by physical destruction of the will; or by the terms of a later will. Remarriage does not automatically disinherit a former spouse named in the first will; a new will must be made.
- A will cannot be determined valid in a court of law if it was written under undue influence, or if fraud or error can be ascertained.
- Most states only require two witnesses, but it is better to have three if at all possible. A beneficiary should *not* be a witness.
- The testator and the witnesses must sign or initial each page in the margin.

 **You *can* write your own will, especially if your estate is worth less than $50,000.**

These are some of the highlights for insuring that a will is valid. If you have questions about writing a will, or have a large or complicated estate, your best bet is to seek advice from a trained, competent professional. A simple will can be drawn up for as little as $100 or $200, with the cost rising as it gets more involved.

Preparing the Will

Whether you write your own will or have an attorney draw it up, here are some general items to consider. Since an attorney usually charges by the hour, it will save both time and money to think through some of these points beforehand.

- BURIAL INSTRUCTIONS: It is important that these be spelled out, particularly if you are going to a foreign country (and always carry a copy of the will with you). The husband of a family cruising in Greece died, and his wife and children had a terrible time getting his body shipped back to the United States so he could be buried in the family plot. Since no will existed giving different instructions, the Greek authorities insisted he be buried according to their laws. They would have recognized a valid will. While this won't necessarily be true in all countries, it still is better to have the instructions with you than to have nothing.
- TRUST PROPERTY: A trust is an arrangement between you and another party (an individual, a trust company, a bank, etc.), giving them the right to control specified portions of your property for the benefit of someone else (your children, for example). This all can be spelled out in a will, or a trust agreement can be established prior to making the will. How it is written can have tax implications. It is a complex area, and any arrangements should be made with professional guidance.
- NAMING AN EXECUTOR: Someone must be designated to handle the settlement of your estate. An alternate executor also should be named, in case the first one dies or decides not to accept the responsibility.
- PERSONAL PROPERTY: Dispose of tangible personal property by separate provisons in the will. Otherwise, under most state laws, it will all go into the bulk of the estate, possibly forcing the executor to sell the property. It is best to specify, by name and relationship, who is to receive the most valuable of your possessions, leaving the balance to a trusted individual to disperse at his/her discretion.

One point to keep in mind if you are far away. When you name the recipient of your boat, camper, microbus or whatever, include a specified amount of cash that will allow them to get it home or pay for shipping or delivery by a professional crew. You wouldn't want to leave the boat to your favorite but young and struggling nephew in Boston, only to have him lose it because he didn't have the money to get to Bora Bora and bring it home. It could sit and rot until the local authorities confiscated it.

 **If you're far from home in a boat, camper or other valuable escape vehicle, make sure to leave enough money so its beneficiary can bring it back home.**

- REAL PROPERTY: Decide whether any solely-owned real estate is to be bequeathed outright, placed in a trust, sold and the proceeds distributed, or the rights to its use given to one beneficiary for their lifetime with ownership going to someone else upon that beneficiary's death (for instance, leaving the use of a house to a second wife, with ownership passing to a child from the first marriage upon the death of the second wife).
- CASH BEQUESTS: When a specific amount of money is left to an individual or a charity, the executor is required to pay that amount first, before any other distribution is made. If the estate is smaller than anticipated at the time of death, it could mean other beneficiaries will receive less than you intended. It is better to state that cash bequests will be paid only if the total estate is above a specified minimum, or state the bequests as percentages or fractions of the total estate.
- IMPLEMENTING THE WILL: It is not a pleasant thought, but people sometimes are lost at sea. Include a provision stating that if you are reported missing, the will is not to be implemented until a specified number of days have passed. You could conceivably drift around for weeks in a life raft or spend months wandering in some wilderness before being rescued, only to come home to discover that all your money and possessions have been disposed of by an efficient executor.

**Remember, cash bequests are paid first. If you're uncertain of how big your estate will be at your death, you can specify bequests as a percentage of your estate.**

A Sample Will

The will shown at the end of the chapter was drawn up by Steve Bloch, an attorney in Virginia *and* a sailor. It is shown only as an example of a "typical" will that might be written for a childless cruising couple, or for someone with limited assets. It is not intended that it be copied verbatim by anyone wanting to write their own will; it is offered for use only as a reference guide.

Maintaining the Will

The original will should be kept in a safe, secure place. Most often this is a safe deposit box belonging to your attorney. Two copies of the will should be made, one to keep with you—and obviously someone else should know where it is—and the other one left with a trusted friend or relative—whoever would be the first person informed of your death. This is done so any special provisions can be put into action immediately. Both copies should have a letter attached stating where the original is located.

Always carry a copy of your will with you and leave a second copy with a trusted relative or friend, preferably whoever will first learn of your death.

One final point: banks automatically freeze single-named bank accounts and safe deposit boxes when the holder dies. They will not freeze joint accounts or boxes held in more than one name. That's why it is a good idea for couples to have joint accounts, even if they each have one they consider as their own. In the event of the death of one spouse, the other will have access to all cash immediately, without having to wait for probate. Adding the person who will become executor to your account will give them access to monies needed for burial or other immediate expenses.

Banks freeze single-name accounts whenever the person dies. It's a good idea for couples to have joint accounts to ensure immediate access to cash.

LAST WILL AND TESTAMENT
OF

I, _____, of _____, being of full age and sound and disposing mind and memory, do freely make, publish and declare this to be my Last Will and Testament, hereby revoking any and all wills and codicils that I have previously made.

ARTICLE I

It is my express desire and wish that my earthly remains be disposed of by cremation. I do not desire a funeral. Any gifts or remembrances should be sent in my name to _____

ARTICLE II

I direct that all my enforceable debts and any expenses incurred as a result of my death and subsequent cremation be paid as soon as possible from my estate and that all estate and inheritance taxes and other governmental charges assessed by reason of my death be paid out of the residue of my estate generally, without need for proration or reimbursement from or charging any person for any part of the taxes and charges so paid. Notwithstanding this provision, I direct that any mortgages on real or personal property owned by me at the time of my death be paid in any manner and at the full discretion of my Executor.

ARTICLE III

If I become unconscious, incoherent or otherwise unable to respond to normal human discourse and it is recommended by attending physicians to rely upon and/or attach extraordinary mechanical, electrical or other life support systems to my body in attempting to preserve my human existence when there is no reasonable medical probability of recovery, and/or if such systems have been previously relied upon or attached and there later becomes no reasonable medical probability of recovery, it is my express desire and wish that such systems not be relied upon and/or attached to my body, and that I be permitted to live in normal course with ordinary medical treatment.

ARTICLE IV

I am married to _____, and all references in this Will to my spouse are to him/her. We currently have no children now living. (Or include names of children and birthdates).

ARTICLE V

Except as otherwise specifically noted, I have made no provision herein for the benefit of my relatives, including but not limited to my mother and father, my brother(s) and my sister(s), not because of lack of love or affection but because they have ample property of their own, or are otherwise able to care for themselves.

ARTICLE VI

I bequeath all of my tangible personal property to my (wife/ husband), _____, if he/she survives me, including my/our sailing vessel known as _____, Documentation No. _____, her gear and equipment, any and all property either owned jointly or by me alone, all our tools, all my clothing, jewelry, household goods, personal effects, automobiles, and all other tangible personal property owned by me at my death, not otherwise specifically bequeathed herein, including cash on hand or on deposit. (Camper or RV can be substituted for boat).

ARTICLE VII

To the individuals and institutions listed below, I bequeath the following:

A. To my (Relationship), _____, if he/she survives me, (name item desired), if owned by me at the time of my death.

B. To my (Relationship), _____, if he/she survives me, (name item desired), if owned by me at the time of my death.

C. To my great-uncle, Klem Kadiddlehopper, if he survives me, my 1903 Hupmobile automobile, if owned by me at the time of my death.

ARTICLE VIII

If my spouse, _____, and I die under such circumstances that there is insufficient evidence to determine the order of our deaths, or if he/she dies within a period of 180 days after the date of my death, then all provisions made herein to or for his/her benefit shall be void; and my estate shall be administered and distributed in all respects as though my said spouse had not survived me.

ARTICLE IX

In the event my spouse predeceases me, I bequeath the following:

A. To _____, of _____, _____, if he survives me, our sailing vessel _____, Documentation No. _____, all of her gear and the tools on board, plus $5,000 cash to assist in transporting her to his home port.

B. To my good friend and mentor, Daffy Duck of Hollywood, California, if he survives me, my 40-acre plot of land located in Texas, U.S.A., commonly known as Downtown Dallas.

C. I give and bequeath all remaining funds, including cash on hand or on deposit, all tangible personal property, all real estate, all royalties from book or other publications, and any other assets arising from my estate, to _____.

ARTICLE X

I nominate and appoint my husband/wife as Executor/Executrix of my Will. Should he/she be unable or unwilling to serve as Ex-

ecutor, I then nominate and appoint _____of
_____, _____substi-
tute Executor. Neither the Executor nor the substitute Executor
shall be required to give bond or other security for the faithful
discharge of that office.

The Executor and the substitute Executor shall have complete
discretion and authority to sell, transfer, mortgage, lease and con-
vey at public or private sale, for cash or credit, all of my property
and estate of every kind and description upon such terms and
conditions as may be deemed advisable, to make distribution to the
beneficiaries hereunder in cash or in kind or in undivided interests
in the property owned by me, and to execute all necessary instru-
ments and do all other things required for the convenient and
expeditious administration of my estate. Any mortgage or lease
made by my Executor or substitute Executor may extend beyond
the term of my estate.

ARTICLE XI

Although it is my understanding that my husband/wife is or may
be executing his/her Will at or about the same time as the execution
of my Will, it is not my nor our intention that such Wills shall be
construed to be mutual, reciprocal, contractual, or dependent upon
one another, even though certain provisions are reciprocal.

IN WITNESS WHEREOF I have hereunto subscribed my name
and published and declared this as my Last Will and Testament on
this _____day of _____, 1983, at _____,
_____, and I have initialed each page of this
instrument in the left margin to identify the page as part of this
will.

_____

The foregoing instrument was on the date thereof, by _____
subscribed and declared to be his/her Will, in the presence of us,
who at his/her request, and in his/her presence, and in the presence
of each other, do sign the same as witness thereto.

_____, residing at _____

_____, residing at _____

_____, residing at _____

GLOSSARY

Beneficiary: Someone who receives benefits from a will or a trust.

Executor: Someone appointed to settle and administer the provisions of the will.

Intestate: Dying without a valid will.

Personal Property: Any property other than real property; property that can be moved.

Probate: The settling of an estate by the Probate Court.

Real Property: Real estate; land, and any fixed improvements on it (houses, barns, etc.).

Testator: Someone who makes a valid will.

Trustee: An individual or company that handles and disburses trust property to the beneficiaries.

Epilogue

The escape is over. It's back to the workaday world. For a few, it never happens. They go on and on, stopping occasionally to work, but never really return to their old ways. Others return physically, but never make it back psychologically, and are soon off once more. For most, however, the escape does end; sometimes permanently, sometimes until the children are grown or retirement comes.

Upon first returning, there's the joy at seeing family and friends again, the excitement of welcome home parties, stories to tell, gossip to catch up on. But when the realization that it really *is* over sets in, the ensuing depression can be tough to deal with.

The best remedy is to get involved in something new—finding a new house or fixing up the old apartment, searching for a rewarding job, starting up a new business or getting back into the old one. For some, the remedy takes the form of planning the next escape or even building a new boat.

Those who know the return to workaday life is only temporary seem to have the easiest time adjusting. If they're sailors, often they continue to live aboard, sometimes for years. By living aboard they remain in the sailing/cruising environment, secure in the knowledge that they *have* been cruising and will do so again—it's just another "work stop" regardless of how long it lasts. They still live in the home that carried them adventuring. It may be tied to a dock, but they know how easy it is to cast off the lines, maybe just for a weekend out at anchor. But it doesn't matter, they haven't lost their mobility, or their momentum. Conversely, those who sever all ties with their escape often have the hardest time adjusting.

But returning to a fixed, middle-class life doesn't have to be a stifling experience. A big project such as renovating an old house or building from the ground up can be exciting and all-consuming. And a few will find that escaping wasn't what they expected, anyway. For them, the transition is relatively easy.

Phyllis Solakian, in a *Cruising World* magazine article, explains that after two years and 3,000 miles of cruising, it was the inconveniences that finally drove her off the boat. She grew tired of having to conserve water, of not being able to shower every day in a clean bathroom, of the compact storage that made it difficult to get at things she wanted. She wanted to be able to sleep all night without worrying about the anchor dragging. Phyllis says that at first the inconveniences were accepted as part of cruising, but eventually they became irritants. For her, moving ashore was easy.

Many escape artists like the Solakians keep their boat, camper or other escape machine. They still enjoy taking off on weekends. Or they view their periodic vacations as mini-escapes. Frequent escapes on a small scale, many discover, is the best way of easing the transition to a more settled life.

Index